Head, Heart and Hands

A journey of personal transformation

Álvaro González Alorda

ISBN: 9798635980880

Alvaro González Alorda is managing partner of **emergap**, a consulting firm specialised in transforming organisations. In the last fifteen years, he has worked with more than one hundred companies in thirty countries of Europe and America. He is professor of **Headspring** (by Financial Times & IE Business School) and visiting professor of business schools in Chile, Argentina, Uruguay, Peru, Colombia, Mexico, United States, United Kingdom and Spain. He was educated at the **University of Navarre, IESE Business School** and at **Harvard Business School.** He is author of the bestsellers **Los Próximos 30 años** and **The Talking Manager.**

linkedin.com/in/alvarogonzalezalorda
facebook.com/agalorda
instagram.com/agalorda
twitter.com/agalorda
#HeadHeartandHands

To all those whom I have had the
fortune to be able to accompany
on any part of their journey

Index

.

Introduction

I took a sabbatical in the summer of 2007. I had been consulting for two years – at that time under the guidance of Luis Huete, Professor at the IESE business school – and I perceived such a disproportionate gap between my knowledge and the challenges facing me each day that I decided to spend two months entirely dedicated to studying change management and innovation. I went to Boston, I registered at the Baker Library of Harvard Business School, I selected a dozen books and I spent the summer reading. In the morning, in the library, and in the afternoon, reclining on a wooden platform over the Charles River. Before dinner, I would row for an hour to digest what I had learned. I didn't obtain any academic distinction, accreditation, or even a cardboard certificate from that experience because I was not enrolled in any official course. But I didn't need one. I was conscious of being there on a research visit for my own purposes.

The inertia of that summer– in fact it started in the University of Navarre, thanks to some talented professors with whom I was lucky enough to be able to achieve an academic education - has lasted for thirteen years, during which I have read more than three hundred books on a wide variety of subjects and innumerable articles, mainly concerning transformation. Together with working as a consultant, - at first with small companies, then mid-sized and, now, mainly large companies, -all this has turned into a circle of learning that makes you feel permanently like a twenty year old university student whose brain is like a sponge, whose pockets are empty and whose heart is full with dreams.

Two years after that summer sabbatical, I wrote *The next thirty years*. Re-reading it makes me smile at the verve and daring with which I wrote, like a pony that leaps the fencing of the pound to gallop around the fields. It was a very personal book, in which I described my experience of how learning accelerates under the guidance of a mentor and - through a handful of stories – I set out some ideas on how to plan a professional career that unfurls your talent. The following year, I wrote *The Talking Manager*, on the importance of conversation as a transformation tool, which I have had the opportunity to verify on numerous occasions.

Then, suddenly, I realised that the ink had dried up. Partly because of the increasing amount of consultancy work that we have had at **emergap**, the "boutique" consultancy that I founded with Raúl Lagomarsino, joined later by Ernesto Barrera, Joaquín Trigueros, Juan Carlos Valverde, Rolando Roncancio, John Almandoz and Gonzalo Valseca. And partly because I wanted to gain more experience before writing about what we have learned in these fifteen years of accompanying companies in their transformation processes, a relatively new area, less than a couple of decades old, in which we are all learning as we go.

What have we learned? In the first place, there are three types of company: those which use a discourse of transformation; those whose model for change is very technical, focussed on technological and business transformation, orchestrated from a project office; and those which, on the one hand, have a complete model for transformation, orientated towards the innovation of their current business model, in order to seize new opportunities for growth and, on the other hand, which transform their organisations by developing new competencies in their people, starting with senior management. We have come across very few of this last type of company.

Secondly, we have learned that transformation requires a methodology that is simple, which a frequent battle ground for large companies because they tend to adopt solutions that are complex, due to systemic inertia peculiar to large structures.

And thirdly, that the transformation of a company is only superficial unless a wave of personal transformations of the people in the organisation is set in motion. I am not referring to skin-deep but to in-depth changes: to the development of new competencies, to the creation of new habits, and to character building that is required to assume the responsibilities of leadership. On this issue, rather than two decades of experience, there are almost three thousand years, and giants of the stature of Aristotle and Cicero, classic works that are seldom read by the senior management of companies. The tragedy of numerous organisations acquires the dimensions of a Greek tragedy, precisely, when their leaders have not only not read the classics, but do not read even five books a year, a figure descending progressively since Netflix became popular.

In these fifteen years, we have had the enormous fortune of contributing to the transformation of more than a hundred companies in thirty countries of Europe and America. And we have verified that, even though a business transformation is a formidable challenge, there is nothing more challenging than personal transformation. For this reason we designed the **Programme of Self-development**, orientated at accelerating the personal and professional growth of the leaders of the organisations that we serve.

By delving into the private lives of Sarah and Oliver, this book depicts a journey of personal transformation that is composed of a multitude of personal stories that we have been privileged to observe over the course of the years. It doesn't matter whether you found the book on a shelf dedicated to *management* or to *fiction*. But now that it is in your hands, I invite you to read it first of all from the perspective of your heart. You will always have time to re-read it from the perspective of your head.

PART ONE

Head, Heart and Hands

Application by email to participate in a mentoring programme

good morning... my name's Sarah ... let's make this clear... this is not me. I'm not comfortable talking with strangers and it's not my style to tell the story of my life to a mentor online ... I prefer personal interactions, face to face. And I don't like people on social networks who hide behind a false photo or a drawing. I need to see a person's face to be able to read it ... that's my work, that's my career, reading faces ... but maybe it's too early to open that subject... following the application instructions, here goes a description of my professional career and the reason for my interest in this online mentoring programme: I am sales manager and if nothing goes astray within a year I will be vice president of my company ... they have officially confirmed it ... but Human Resources have put me on the runway and authorised me to do this programme. My company is sophisticated ... they don't tell you how you have to train yourself, they give you the funds and you decide how. In the last decade I have been to several business schools after studying International Business at the Tec in Monterrey... first I went to Madrid to do an MBA at IE, then I did professional development programmes at Harvard and Kellogg and I have been on numerous seminars for acquiring different skills. Now I lead an international project that means that I travel around the world three weeks a month ... so to progress along the development path of my company I need a flexible programme that adapts to my frenetic agenda ... That's what you offer, no? At least, that's what I understood from your website... I was reading your profiles and I liked Oliver's (suggestion, load photos, I like to se the face of my mentor, or at least the surname, to look him up in Linkedin). They say he is demanding

13

and has received positive evaluations, although a negative one, too ... I suppose nobody can please everybody ... I think I'm in the same boat ... I don't like everybody and not everybody likes me .... They have given me that feedback ... they say I am very direct and sometimes my comments to others are hurting ... perhaps it's true, I can't stand inefficiency or lack of accountability ... What else? I am married to Bryan and we have no children. I like dancing... I was tennis champion at school ... I love dogs... Now I've said too much ... I hope it's sufficient for the description you asked for. Ah! I forgot something important ..... I'm from Medellín. I attach my CV. I await instructions. Sarah

19th February | Punta del Este | 09:55
Reply to the application to participate in a mentoring programme

Good morning, Sarah.

Welcome to our Mentoring Programme. I would like to notify you formally that you may consider that your application has been approved, on the basis of your professional profile and your career path, although not due to the way you write, with errors and a degree of informality which is inappropriate for a person of your academic and professional experience.

As you will have seen in our website, the programme lasts for nine months and the way we work is based on two main media of communication:

- A monthly conversation by videoconference.
- Weekly interactions on our online platform, whereby which we assign tasks and through which you should publish your achievements in self-development.

Our mentoring model is based on three principles:

1. You are the protagonist of your own self-development. This responsibility cannot be delegated either to your company's Human Resources team, or to us. Our role is to accompany you throughout this process in order to help you to identify your development challenges, to select the competencies that you wish to work on, to translate them into specific projects and to implement them with discipline.

2. The purpose of this mentoring programme is to accompany you in developing competencies (sets of habitual behaviour that are observable and measurable), to incorporate and assimilate new habits and to build the character that is necessary to assume leadership responsibilities. Personal transformation is not achieved by attending a couple of courses each year – that alone is simply academic tourism - or by listening to motivational talks.

3. The quality of your leadership depends on the quality of your mentoring. The difference between a mere manager and a leader is that the former focuses all his energy on day to day operations, whereas the latter incorporates another two responsibilities on his agenda: strategy and people development. A good assessment of the degree to which you have taken advantage of this programme will be precisely you capacity to implement this ethos of mentoring and self-development in your own team.

Allow me to introduce myself: I am Oliver. In attention to your express request, I have been assigned as your mentor. I was born in Windsor (England). I graduated at Oxford University and have worked in the business world for more than three decades. Now, I live for most of the year in Punta del Este (Uruguay) with my wife, Valentina. My two daughters, Claire and Alison, live in London and in Madrid. I will soon be a grandfather. I also like dogs; I have three of them.

From now on we will communicate through a private channel on our mentoring platform, which supports written and audio texts, file attachments, and videoconferences. Only you and I will have access to this channel. All our communications will be confidential.

You will see my face during our first videoconference (already planned for 28th February), for which reason it would be very useful if you would take the DISC personality test and also if you would publish on the platform your reply to the question: What is Sarah's personality? Try to observe yourself as though you were a third party who knows you well and reply from that perspective.

Yours sincerely

Oliver

22nd February | Boston | 01:30
Text message publish on the platform

Dear Oliver ... I was on the point of leaving the programme ... without ever having started. Your message was very hard on me ... but I forwarded it to my friend Andrea and ... I couldn't believe it ... she sided with you! Can writing really be so important in a world that has evolved to emoticons and audio messages? Anyway, to avoid causing more disgust, Andrea recommended an app that corrects spelling and grammar errors. It has corrected half a dozen in this paragraph ... I hope this improves our relation ... still non-existent.

Talking about the DISC test, I did it years ago but I can't remember what came out. I have done it again now and it has left me pensive... It seems like I have a personality clearly pointing to Dominance and Influence. In general, I think it's an accurate diagnosis, although I don't agree with all the traits it gives me... According to the Dominance profile, I am determined, competitive, and demanding, but also distant, individualist and bossy. And according to the Influence profile, I am sociable, talkative and passionate, but also indiscrete, inconstant and disordered. Bryan thinks it's a portrait of me... but I think people have a degree of complexity than a simple test can't capture. For me it's as artificial as classifying animals by the number of legs they have...

So, let's go to your question: *What is Sarah's personality?*

Sarah isn't the typical person you can classify in two categories... I actually think she has a liquid personality that adapts to the context and to people. When she was little her mother said to her: "With you, my girl, you never know which way you are going to react"... And in fact, sometimes I left home through the window, climbing a tree, not to escape but from love of adventure. Yes, she is also an adventurer.... For years she spent part of her holidays in the Colombian Amazon jungle, helping with the building of a school in an indigenous community, something that scared stiff her friends from Medellin, who preferred to go on cruises in the Caribbean or to go shopping in Miami, not that Sarah is opposed to those activities because she also practised them a lot ... she has a collection of more than sixty pairs of shoes, which now and again give rise to arguments with her husband Bryan, who is her antithesis, or complements her perfectly if you like, because he is amiable, serene, sensible and well organised. Sarah owes to this latter quality a significant reduction in the number of missed flights due to leaving her passport at home... he always says goodbye with a familiar routine: "Have a good trip, darling. Keys? Handbag? Passport?" But don't get the wrong impression, one thing is for Sarah to live at a fast pace and quite another that she doesn't pay attention to things ... her team fears her because she remembers everything, especially numbers, and she can fulminate them if they don't give her the right figure.... That's when you can see the veins in her forehead and a storm bursts. although it is usually a summer storm, noisy but short. What else? Sarah likes working, she enjoys sports and she makes friends easily. Some say she is very intense.

I hope this is some use.

Sarah

28th February | Boston – 16:07 | Punta del Este – 17:07
Videoconference

—Hi, Oliver, qué pena con usted, / what a pity /shame with you??? forgive me being late, a meeting just ran on.
—Hullo Sarah, pleased to meet you. You can treat me without any formality. I will soon be a grandfather, but I'm not so old.
—Yes sir.
—I have read what you published on the platform last night. Bearing in mind that it is not your style to tell the story of your life online to a mentor, you did a good job with the description of your character. It provides many details that help me to begin to get to know you. Thank you for being so frank.
—Not at all. Sorry I sent it a bit late but this week I returned from a long trip and my agenda got complicated yesterday and I finished up working very late...
—That's alright. I would like to start by emphasizing something important: my only purpose in this mentoring process is to help you to grow as a leader, both in your organisation and in your personal life. We are going to apply a methodology of which the positive impact on you depends

directly on the discipline with which you implement it.

—I know. It was clear from your first message that I am the owner of my self-development.

—That's right. I see that you are elegantly dressed.

—Thank you. What's that got to do with it?

—Your first message wasn't in the same vein. It was full of errors of grammar and style. It was something like appearing in the office with old, dirty clothes.

—OK. I like to be clear and for others to be clear with me. But I'm not sure I'm ready right now for such a crude feedback...

—¿And are you ready to be appointed vice president in a year's time?

—I guess so. They consider me high potential and even the Chairman has spoken to me about that possibility.

—You may well end up there, even without going through this programme, although the chances are that you will achieve it in the same way as so many other people, who reach executive committees with good results as managers, but as mediocre leaders.

—What do you mean?

—We'll come back to that later. For the time being, I simply want to point out that perhaps you have deep-seated, commonplace set of assumptions about what it means to be a leader. In the course of the programme, I will challenge you to identify opportunities to improve and I will suggest mechanisms that will instigate you to pursue excellence.

 —Sounds interesting, but a bit abstract.

—Now let's go to your personality. I would like to know you better. This is the first stage of the mentoring itinerary that we are going to follow.

—And what happens afterwards?

—Knowledge about personality helps to identify possible development challenges. Then I will pass on to you a self-diagnosis test of competencies, so that you can select those competencies on which you wish to work in the course of the programme. And later, those competencies have to be incorporated into projects for personal transformation, which we will follow-up during our interactions on the platform.

—I understand.

—Currently, is there any professional situation that is causing you stress?

—It isn't a situation. It's a person, called Helen.

—What's the matter with Helen?

—Puff, she is the most inflexible person I have ever known. She can't stand discrepancy. We have been working on a project for the past year and I find it really difficult to administer my relationship with her. I have the feeling that she has been trained to contradict me. Not a meeting goes by without her expressing her disagreement with what I say on several occasions. But what most irritates me are those emails with a copy to the boss in which she never fails to take advantage of the opportunity to enumerate with exasperating detail all the risks of implementing the project and the slightest error in my reports. They are usually small details. I don't know why she finds them so important. We have the mandate to implement a new model of consultative sales on a global scale and it's difficult to make any progress with Helen dragging the team down. So I have opted for handling everything with her by email. Because it's obvious that Helen isn't going to change.

—It sounds as if you are bosom enemies.

—Literally.

—Is Helen also at your corporative offices in Boston?

—Yes. Who isn't there is me because I spend my time travelling. And that's part of the problem. Whilst she sits comfortably in her office, indicating problems, one floor away from the Chairman's office, I am working with local teams from country to country, from hotel to hotel, constantly changing time zones, answering emails at night and connecting to videoconferences when I have that sniper aiming at my head with her rifle, firing information that I don't have and sowing

20

doubts about my work. That's what most irritates my nerves, not being able to be there, in the conference room, to be able to read people's faces and to know how to handle the situation.

—I understand. How many people report to you directly?

—Directly, four. One is in Boston, one in London, one in Copenhagen and one in Berlin. And another eight in the corporate structure, distributed between the United States and Europe.

—Which part of your work do you most enjoy?

—I'll answer you with something that happened two weeks ago. On Monday the opportunity arose of presenting an offer to a potential customer in London. They gave us an appointment with the Chairman of the company for the Wednesday, at nine in the morning, something that is completely exceptional. I was in Berlin. I immediately set up a videoconference with three people from my team, I prepared the strategy for the meeting and asked them all to get moving to the airport to take the first available flight to London. One came from Boston, another from Copenhagen, I came from Berlin and another was already in London. We arrived over the course of Tuesday and we got together in the Hyatt Regency Hotel. Each brought the part of the presentation they had prepared, and we fine-tuned and rehearsed it until two in the morning. The following day, the meeting went spectacularly well, and they asked us to present an offer for a three-million-dollar contract. It isn't in the bag, by a long way, but it has raised an opportunity to work with a large new customer. So unexpectedly, that meeting served as a prototype for our new consultative sales model. We left the meeting so exhausted and so excited that to celebrate we went to Scott's, a restaurant that I love. The dynamics and motivation that were generated, that sense of achievement as a team, is the kind of moment I most enjoy.

—What an interesting experience. Which professional competencies have you developed most?

—I think I'm good at getting results, selling, managing

customer relations, leading teams, managing projects and, in general, communication.

—Those competencies sound good for the Commercial Manager. How many emails do you have right now in your inbox? How many still unread?

—Let me see. In the inbox I have 11.123. Unread, 282. But the majority are corporate emails they send you by default. Quite honestly, global organisations are an inexhaustible source of irrelevant communications.

—Now, imagine that, just after ending our videoconference, the CEO asks you to make a presentation tomorrow to the Executive Committee. Three questions. What would be your first reaction? How would you feel tomorrow during the presentation? When would you prepare it? Answer briefly, in a few words.

—My immediate reaction would be to feel a knot in my stomach. At the beginning, I would feel nervous, but after a few minutes, no-one would be able to stop me talking. I would prepare it tonight.

—If you had to describe your main professional challenge, how would you summarise it?

—To implement on an international scale a new commercial model based on consultative sales and to get a diversified and delocalised team to integrate it into their daily work, and to develop a more fluid collaborative dynamic with other areas of the organisation.

—That's not bad. Given the nature of the challenge, what is required on your part, more technical knowledge or more leadership competencies?

—I would say twenty per cent technical knowledge and eighty per cent leadership competencies.

—More than a management challenge it would appear to be a transformation challenge. Let's move on to another question. Who is your best friend? And why?

—Oliver, I'm telling you the story of my life. I hope it is of some use. Quite honestly, I had expected other things from this mentoring. Nobody asks me these questions.

—Not even your boss?

—My vice president asks me lots of questions. Too often, I think. But they are practically all about how my project is progressing and about results.

—In my case, I only want to get to know you better. Are my question uncomfortable for you?

—Not at all. I don't know where this process is leading me, but for the moment I find it interesting. Interesting and enjoyable.

—I'm glad to hear it. Although there will be less enjoyable moments. Your best friend?

—Undoubtedly my best friend is Andrea. She is a friend from childhood. In fact, she's like a sister. She is the most sensible person you can imagine. She hasn't had an easy life. She lost her mother in a traffic accident when she was twelve and she had to take on looking after herself, her two small brothers, and also her father, in a way. The poor man didn't recover from the death of his wife. Until the accident, Andrea spent her time at my house, and we were together all the time. From that moment, it was the opposite; I started going to her house to help with domestic chores. Since then we have been very united, and we are in touch almost every day. Andrea is married. She lives in Medellin and she works as the director of a school in one of the poorest areas of the city. She could be the finance manager of a multinational. I think, in fact, that she's the most intelligent person I know. But she has a calling to help others that I find admirable and, sometimes, incomprehensible.

—I understand. Tell me about something endearing that you remember from your infancy.

—You want to go that far back?

—As far as you will allow me.

—At home we had a tradition. Each year there was a trip for boys, organised by my father and my brother, and another one for girls, organised by my mother and me. When I was nine, my mother took me on a boat trip in the Amazon. But don't think of us rowing a canoe. It was a small cruiser with a capacity for about ten people, with all the comforts and luxuries that were more exuberant than the jungle. At night, when everyone had retired to their cabins, my mother and I went up to the main deck and lay down to watch the stars. One night, my mother invited me to dream of what my life would be like....

—And?

—... God!

—Are you alright?

—Let's leave it there.

—Yes, fine. Tell me three values that are important for you.

—Authenticity, work and ... can they be just two for the moment?

—There's no hurry. About authenticity, that was clear to me from your application. We had never received such a defiant message with our online mentoring model, before having the chance to experience it. Can you go further into why work is such an important value for you?

—That's something I owe mainly to my grandmother, although it's painful not to be able to say the same about my mother ... My grandmother lived form the day she was born until she died in a beautiful country estate in Llanogrande, about an hour from Medellin. She could have had a comfortable life, but she spent it helping agricultural workers in the area. Apart from giving them work and paying them properly, she set up a flower farm for them, she taught their children to read ... she even invited them to celebrate Christmas with their families on the estate. She was a well loved woman. She was always helping others. She cooked very well. I never saw her resting. I think I have inherited that active spirit.

—How did you meet Bryan?

—When I was living in Madrid, when I was doing my MBA at IE, I was invited to a party at the one of my friends' house, which was an attic in the street called María de Molina. It had

24

a small terrace with fantastic views of the gardens of the French Ambassador's residence. I don't know what we drank nor how much, but the idea occurred to me of letting a piece of paper with a heart drawn on it and with the text "I love you" float down to the street. Quite by chance, Bryan was passing and saw the paper and heard the music and laughter. He came up to the attic, knocked on the door, showed me the piece of paper and winked at me.

—It's hard to believe …!

—Every time I tell the story, I think the same thing.

—That's called having a good aim. You said that his qualities make him a perfect match for you.

—That's for sure. He's the typical, quiet Californian and I am always at top speed.

—Working non-stop?

—Yup. Bryan says I need to rest and disconnect.

—How do you rest? What do you do to disconnect?

—My therapy for disconnecting is called Netflix, but it's tricky, because it deprives me of hours of sleep.

—How many hours do you sleep?

—Between six and seven, but nearer six, - I know, - it isn't enough. Bryan is a doctor and he reminds me by throwing scientific studies at me about the terrible effects on health of the lack of sleep.

—And how well do you sleep?

—Badly. I think I'm in a permanent state of alert. I live against the clock. I have an interminable list of things pending in my head.

—Do you practice any sport?

—I always travel with my running shoes, but I often return home without having used them. I'm inconstant.

—That is very typical in personalities of Influence. What are you reading?

—Reading? Well, I read the news and stock exchange information. In our business you have to be informed about the markets.

—Any book?

—Not long ago they gave me a book called Homo Sapiens, or something like that, but I have only read ten or twelve pages.

—Sarah, it's time to be closing. In our next conversations I will take up again some aspects of what has come out today. But now I would like to focus on one: the importance of reading. You are not engaged in manufacturing. Your professional performance does not depend on the strength of your arms or the capacity to carry a heavy load on your back. Rather, you spend your time "mindfacturing". So, given the nature of the challenges you have, the quality of your leadership depends to a enormous extent on the vitality of your intellect; on your conceptual affluence; on your capacity to process complex information and to diagnose; on your competencies in communicating; on your skill in swiftly detecting the talent and personality of people; in other words, on your capacity to navigate through the National Geographic of the human spirit. From this perspective, the habit of reading is a fabulous tool for developing all those competencies. And to read twenty books a year is a reasonable rhythm to cultivate them.

[your performance as leader does not depend on the strength of your arms or the capacity to carry a heavy load on your back. Rather, you spend your time "mindfacturing". So the level of your leadership depends directly on the vitality of your intellect; on your conceptual affluence; on your capacity to process complex information and to synthesise; on your capacity to think critically and not be drawn by superficial, populist slogans; on your competencies in communicating both verbally and in writing; on your skill in swiftly detecting the talent and personality of people; in other words, on your capacity to navigate through the National Geographic of the human spirit. From this point of view, the habit of reading and studying (books and articles, but also videos, podcasts, documentaries, etcetera) are fabulous tools of personal growth. Today, however, we run the risk of reducing our intellectual diet to serials offered by a platform such as Netflix, a potentially addictive self service for fast-food.]

—Just a moment, Oliver. I don't think I have read twenty books ... in all my life!
—It's never too late to start. Yes I know that it sound like too many, but it isn't an extraordinary number. I know many people who read considerably more. Imagine for a moment that this year you read twenty books. And net year, twenty more. And the following year, another twenty. Where will you be in five years? Where will you be in a hundred books time? How much will you have expanded your knowledge? How much will you have gained in the interior strength you need as a leader? Where will your capacity to inspire others be? Think about it.
—It sounds good and I will think about it . But I warn you that I tried to read years ago and I got bored.
—Perhaps you chose the wrong book. I have in fact come with a suggestion for you: The 7 Habits, by Steven R. Covey. It is a classic that has helped millions of people to adjust their professional focus and bring it in line with their purpose in life.
—Sounds promising, that book.
—I'm glad to hear it. I think you will like it. We will have a conversation by videoconference again in a month's time, but I would like to agree now on how you are going to advance in the next four weeks. Our mentoring methodology prescribes that every week you should publish on the platform at least one of your self-development achievements. Always make a note of the achievement with a #hashtag, so that later on we can find them quickly and review them. So let me propose the following: In weeks one and two, publish a substantial personal reflection induced by your reading of The 7 Habits. In week three, carry out the self-diagnosis of competencies that I will send you and publish your conclusions. We will comment on all this during

the videoconference of week four. Do you agree?
—I agree.
—Fine. I hope all goes well for you.
—Just a moment, Oliver. How old are you?
—Fifty-six.
—You look younger.
—That's very kind of you.
—Thank you for the conversation. It leaves me with a lot to think about and a lot of tasks!
—Not so many. But they require discipline. Talking about discipline, today you connected to the videoconference seven minutes late. Henceforth, I expect you to be punctual.
—Sorry. I promise I'll be punctual.
—Thank you in advance. Have a good week.
—Same to you. Ciao.

9th March | Punta del Este | 08:16
Text message published on the platform

Good morning, Sarah,

I see that in the first week you haven't met your commitment to publish on the platform a reflection about the book *The 7 Habits*. I am concerned about your performance in this programme and I invite you reconsider if you really want to do it. To do it seriously, I mean. If you don't, you are still in time to leave. Oliver.

9th March | Copenhagen | 14:33
Audio message published on the platform

Hi, Oliver, I have just seen your message. You are right and, although I have no excuse, let me explain that last week was just crazy. My boss called an extraordinary meeting on Thursday and I had to stay in Boston and put back my trip to

Copenhagen. I finally flew in here on Sunday, which Bryan didn't like very much because he had to go alone to a dinner at one of our friends' home. Anyway. I started the book *The 7 Habits*, by the way, but I have hardly read the introduction. I promise that I will read for a couple of hours tonight and send you my reflection. Ciao.

10th March | Copenhagen | 02:22
Text message published on the platform

Good evening, Oliver,

«There's so much to do. There's so little time. I feel under pressure and I am in a hurry all day, everyday, seven days a week. I have taken courses on time management and I have tried half a dozen different planning systems. They helped a bit, but I still don't feel that I am living the happy, productive and peaceful life that I want to live. »

I have selected this sentence from the book, although I could have selected many others, because it seems as though Steven Covey wrote *The 7 Habits* thinking of me, in 1989! I can't understand why I haven't read it until now, or why no professor recommended it to me at university, or why none of my bosses has ever mentioned it, or why it isn't basic reading in the leadership courses I have done... Who's responsible for this?

After reading your message this morning (I'm beginning to understand why there are people who don't like your style...), this afternoon I left the office early (although at this time of year Copenhagen is so dark that it might have been 11 o'clock at night), I went to the hotel and asked room service to bring a *Club Sandwich* to my room, and I concentrated on reading and read as far as habit number three. For the time being, these are my reflections, in answer to the two key questions of the book:

—*"What specific thing could you do (something you are not doing now) that, if you did it habitually, would have a tremendously positive effect on your personal life?"*

—Become reconciled with my mother.... But I think it's too complex a challenge for it to be specific. And it's a door that I don't want to open... So let's put something more realistic: sleep at least seven hours every day.

—*"What specific thing in your business or professional life would produce similar results?"*

—Keep my inbox up to date, so that I don't have to stay up every night to reply to unattended messages.

In addition to reflecting, I have also taken a decision... ask my team to read Covey's book.

I hope this is useful to you, Oliver. I don't know why I am telling you such personal things... perhaps because you appear to me to be discreet, with experience and reliable. At least, that's the way you seemed to be during our videoconference.

Good night. Today, for sure, I won't sleep seven hours...

Sarah

10th March | Punta del Este | 08:45
Text message published on the platform

Good morning, Sarah,

May I congratulate you for the frankness with which you are deepening your diagnosis. This is a first critical step in breaking out of mediocrity and advancing towards excellence; both personal and professional. Dimensions begin to appear, such as the relationship with your mother or, presumably, your lack of system in the use of digital tools which, - together with the diagnosis of competencies next week -,may well serve to define your development challenges. The effort you are making to write correctly also draws my attention. A satisfactory effort, perhaps shared with th Grammarly app.

Your question about who is responsible for your not having read a book as valuable as *The 7 Habits*, and many others, has an answer: every time that a university graduates a university student who doesn't read, it becomes an accomplice to fraud, the fraud of producing mere technicians without the human discernment to be able to understand – or contribute to solving – the enormous range of challenges in today's world. Challenges that require integral solutions, with an anthropological basis, and not just applying patches, whether social, economic, political or technological, like someone updating an app by added a few lines of source code. In the second row of the dock for this fraud sit the professors who didn't know how to infect instiltheir students with the passion for reading, perhaps because the excessive time spent on administering has withered their intellectual vitality. And in the front row, those students who haven't found time and space to read in this era of digital distractions.

How about starting today to sleep at least seven hours? May I suggest that you download Habitify, an app that helps to form habits. It can be programmed to remind you that it is time to go to bed, or to plan a daily time for reading, amongst other uses. Every day it will ask you if you have met your commitments and it also gives you statistics on the level of your compliance.

Oliver

15th March | Boston | 18:48
Audio message published on the platform

Oliver, the week has flown by, I am back in Boston and I

haven't read your message until now. I will download Habitify and I'll let you know how next week goes. I haven't got much further with the book. Tonight, I will give it another push. Ciao.

16th March | Punta del Este | 09:18
Text message published on the platform

Good morning, Sarah,

This week is critical in our mentoring process. Here is the link from which you can access the test for self-diagnosis of competencies. [emergap.com/en/diagnosis/] It will take you approximately sixty minutes to complete.

There are twelve competencies which we call "Transformation Competencies" and which in our experience are crucial to induce change with speed and in depth. Why?

In any organisation there are three dynamics that vertebrate practically all its activity: personal conversations, collective conversations (or meetings) and communication through digital tools. As you will see, these twelve competencies, in different degrees, impact the quality in these three environments, which become particularly critical in transformation processes.

You will find a definition of each competency in the link and, for each of them, a list of traits that will help you to evaluate you degree of development and assign yourself a grade.

COMPETENCES

STRATEGY

1 DIAGNOSIS & DECISION

2 PROJECT DESIGN

3 AGILE EXECUTION

LEADERSHIP

4 INTEGRITY

5 CLOSENESS

6 FEEDBACK

COLLABORATION

11 MANAGEMENT OF MEETINGS & WORKSHOPS

10 DIGITAL TOOLS

12 MATRIX INFLUENCE

COMMUNICATION

9 EFFECTIVE PRESENTATIONS

8 WRITTEN SKILLS

7 VERBAL & NON-VERBAL SKILLS

In order to achieve a transformation successfully, these 12 TRANSFORMATION COMPETENCES must be attained by the leaders of the organisation.

These are sets of BEHAVIOUR, not traits of personality or temperament. They are OBSERVABLE: the extent of development, progress and learning can be evaluated. And they are HABITUAL: they are incorporated as habits into everyday activity.

emergap

33

During our first videoconference, you told me that your major professional challenge is currently "to implement on an international scale a new commercial model, based on consultative sales". In order to achieve it, it would not appear that traditional management competencies are sufficient. It's a challenge that requires transformation competencies. Try to look at the model of competencies from this angle.

In order to share with you a common conceptual framework, I ought to point out that competencies are sets of behaviour; they are not traits of personality or temperament. Nor is a competency a body of knowledge. Competencies are orientated to action. They are observable. The degree to which they have been acquired, your progress, your learning, can be evaluated, although some are more difficult to evaluate than others. And they are habitual, they have been incorporated into the person's daily activity. The acquisition of a new competency implies the acquisition of new habits.

The deployment of new capacities in an organisation builds on the individual competencies of each person. So that in order to install a new capacity in an organisation, such as, for example, consultative sales, it is absolutely necessary for the people involved to acquire certain competencies.

I also pass on to you the scale we use in the diagnosis, which is designed to provoke a healthy discomfort.

> **Excellent** | Shows a world class development of the competency. You have studied and applied it so well that you could almost write books or give talks about it.

> **Good** | You are a unanimous point of reference for this competency in the organisation. You are frequently requested to help others to acquire it.

> **Average** | The competency is in active process of development,

but the degree of acquisition means you are not a reference in your organisation.

Bad | You do not have the competency or show noticeable shortages in developing it.

Once you answer all the questions, it will give you a report with the degree of development of each competency and will offer you some recommendations.

I would suggest that you also ask for feedback from some people who know you well about how they see you in respect of these twelve competencies.

I will be awaiting the publication of you reflections on the diagnosis before 21st March. Our next videoconference is planned for 25th March.

Oliver

20th March | Boston | 22:03
Text message published on the platform

Oof... Oliver, if the aim of the self-diagnosis of competencies is to produce discomfort... you've hit the bulls-eye!

I attach the general result that I have obtained in each competency and a selection of the behaviours in which I think I have more opportunity for improvement.

1. DIAGNOSIS AND DECISION - Average

—In a diagnostic process, I do not first go through a divergence phase (open various options) before entering a convergence phase (prioritizing the most relevant).

—I spend the same time in all the dimensions of a problem and can overwhelm others with irrelevant activities.

—I make decisions quickly to avoid the hassle of debating with others.

2. PROJECT DESIGN - Average

—Faced with a new strategic challenge, I find it difficult to anchor it quickly in a specific project, establishing specific and measurable objectives.

—I do not quickly identify the key activities of a project to manage its interdependencies with the different areas of the organisation.

—I do not make sure that the initial requirements of the project are defined precisely, making it easier for the project to start with a clear north.

3. AGILE EXECUTION - Average

—In the projects that I lead, I do not maintain the macro vision and a strategic leadership, and I end up falling into micro-management.

—I don't plan with enough foresight and end up "putting out fires" in the short term.

—I easily delay project follow-up meetings when conflicts arise on my agenda.

4. INTEGRITY - Good

—I do not reflect enough on the values that underlie my life to try to incorporate them consistently into my daily behavior.

—I am so critical of people who do not share my values or opinions that I close myself to dialogue with them and try to understand their perspective.

—I let myself be carried away by behaviors that immediately satisfy me but are not aligned with my values.

5. CLOSENESS - Average

—My way of expressing myself is perceived as abrupt and cutting.

—I put little effort to connect with personalities very different from mine, making my relationship with them difficult.

—I tend to communicate with my team through emails and messages rather than through conversations.

6. FEEDBACK - Bad

—I focus so much on the negatives and the shortcomings of others that I find it hard to see their positive qualities.

—I correct others in public.

—Too often I give the same person feedback on the same issue, sometimes in a complaining tone, losing the effectiveness of the message.

—I don't ask for feedback. And when they give it to me, I find it hard to accept criticism.

7. VERBAL & NON-VERBAL COMMUNICATION - Average

—Before I speak at a meeting, I do not organize and structure my ideas, in writing if necessary, to ensure the clarity of my message.

—When I take the floor, I find it difficult to conclude, "I go into a loop" and end up repeating the same idea several times.

—I don't project my voice hard, using my rib cage, and I end up screaming and forcing my throat.

8. WRITTEN COMMUNICATION - Bad

—I do not check my texts carefully so that they do not come out with misprints, misspellings and grammatical errors.

—I write as I speak, using excessively colloquial expressions.

—I do not usually articulate my messages through a sequence of paragraphs that responds to a logical and clear structure, in order to facilitate their understanding.

9. EFFECTIVE PRESENTATIONS - Bad

—I abuse my ability to improvise and I don't spend enough time preparing well for my public speeches.

—I use more slides than necessary, which makes me go beyond the established time and end up telling the content in a hasty way.

—I always present in the same way, without adapting to the type of audience or changing my tactics when something is not working.

10. DIGITAL TOOLS - Bad

—I excessively use email and WhatsApp without taking advantage of the potential of new professional communication tools.

—I don't set up digital tools in an advanced way to improve my productivity. For example: email rules, personalization of notifications, etc.

—I respond impulsively to the different alerts and notifications that appear on my electronic devices, interrupting my work.

—Communication with my team jumps without criteria from platform to platform (email, WhatsApp, etc.), generating disorder and contributing to losing the traceability of the information.

11. MANAGEMENT OF MEETINGS AND WORKSHOPS - Average

—I do not use different methodologies to manage different types of meetings: project monitoring, ideation, team integration, etc.

—I am late at the beginning and at the end of meetings or workshops.

—During meetings or workshops, I perform multitasking (email, WhatAspp, etc.) and sometimes I leave the meeting to take calls.

—I tend to organize face-to-face meetings for which a video conference would have been sufficient.

12. MATRIX INFLUENCE - Good

—I make decisions that involve other areas without sufficiently weighing how they will affect them.

—When I need to get something critical from other areas of the organisation, I tend to use hierarchical coercion.

—I do not assign enough authority to the people on my team to make their own decisions without waiting for my approval.

Oliver, although I don't think that all those aspects are 100% representative of my behaviour, I have selected them because they have made me think about opportunities to improve. By the way, I haven't had time to ask for feedback from people who know me. For the time being, I'm going to ask Andrea because she has very good judgement.

Sarah

—Hi, Oliver, how are you?

—Fine, thank you. And how are you?

—Just arrived in London and punctual for our videoconference. Something British is rubbing off on me!

—I'm glad to hear it. How many days will you be staying?

—I'll be working with the team here from now until Friday, when I fly to Copenhagen.

—I imagine that you must have earned the platinum card, or perhaps it's titanium.

—I'm afraid that at this rate they'll be giving me one of kryptonite.

—Yes! Indeed! Are you able to get some sleep on intercontinental flights?

—What with dinner being served and me watching some film, not much. By the way, the other day I saw The Intern and the characters reminded me of you and me. You have a certain resemblance with Robert de Niro. Haven't they ever told you?

—Never. But it's a good film. But I am not retired. I simply left the corporate world and have changed my professional activity. How is The 7 Habits going?

—It's a struggle for me to advance; not from lack of interest but because I never find the time with so many things to do and so many fields of operations to deal with.

—Sarah, self-development is not another layer of work or additional activity for when you have some free time. It is one of the three basic responsibilities of a leader...

—Yes, yes, I remember; strategy, people development and operations.

—... which you have to learn to incorporate into your everyday activity. Have you tried listening to audio books?

—No, the honest truth is that I haven't.

—I would recommend the application called Audible, from Amazon. With the number of flights you make and the hours you must spend travelling to and from airports, you could make serious inroads into the dearth of your reading.

—Right. I take note.

—Perhaps you would help if you unsubscribed from Netflix.

—Oh sure. The next thing you'll suggest is that I go and live in a convent.

—Do you look after you diet?

—Yes. Except for guzzling chocolate occasionally when I'm feeling down, I follow quite a balanced diet.

—And how would you describe your intellectual diet?

—...

—Well, the first objective of today's videoconference is to identify your development challenges, bearing in mind your personality, your professional experience, your current professional challenge and the possibility that you will be appointed vice president within a year.

—OK.

—If you had to choose two, which would you say your development challenges were?

—I don't know. I suppose that one would be to implement a new model of consultative sales successfully.

—That's not a development challenge. It's a management challenge. Or rather, for transforming the organisation, because it means implanting a new capacity, based on the new competencies that each person in your team will have to acquire.

—In that case, I'm lost. What is a development challenge?

—How are you feeling today to digest some crude feedback?

—Not very well, but I'm curious. So I prefer you to receive it.

—In summary, I would say that you have reached your maximum level of juniority.

—What does that mean?

—It means that if you don't change in some basic dimensions, you will not attain the level of seniority required to be a vice president legitimately and to form part of the executive committee of an organisation.

—I don't know whether I prefer you to leave it there and move on or for you to continue to rub salt in the wound.

—I will take your doubt to mean that I should continue. I'll give you an example. During our interactions, the way you judge Helen draws attention, with those thick strokes of a paintbrush that portray her in such an exaggerated and unreal way. On top of that, you assert that "she isn't going to change".

—In fact, she isn't going to change!

—That statement is inappropriate for a leader, because it reveals that you have lost faith in the human being's capacity of transformation. Anyone. Including oneself. In other words, when you say that Helen isn't going to change, you are in fact saying that you aren't going to change either.

—You have my mind in a stranglehold.

—Some time ago I had in my hands a book by the German philosopher Josef Pieper, who has now died. He puts this brilliantly. "The lover beholds the beloved, not with realism, but with projection."

 Or words to that effect – I am recalling the idea from memory.

—Are you suggesting that I should love Helen?

—I am suggesting that you change that sceptical look for a

transforming look; a look that admits the possibility of change in others. And what is more important, that admits the possibility of change in oneself. I am proposing that you unleash your transforming leadership.

—Sounds wonderful, but I haven't the faintest idea of how to do that.

—For the moment, it's enough for your head to find it reasonable. Later on, for your heart to find it reasonable. And, finally, for your hands to turn it into concrete facts.

—¿Head, heart and hands?

—Remind me not talk about this during our next videoconference.

—Sure. And what other signs of juniority have you noticed in me during our brief encounters?

—Brief, but intense. I admit that your frankness and your authenticity are facilitating my work as mentor considerably.

—Wow...! At last you've recognised something positive in me.

—Although you may not realise right now, I am trying to behold you with projection, because I'm convinced that you can improve a great deal.

—I suppose so, I'm still young.

—Talking about youth, other signs of juniority are the lack of discipline, which shows in your case in your lack of punctuality, your lack of constancy, that manner you have of working as though it were the "night before the exam", your lack of control in the use of digital tools, the deficient way that you relax, your lack of attention to detail in the reports you present...

—Stop. The point is clear.

—Would you agree, then, that in your case, two possible development challenges would be to cultivate a transformation leadership and to gain in discipline?

—A bit excruciating, but I agree.

—That's a good sign.

—Grind it in! How does this continue?

—The strategic challenges are clear, but up in the stratosphere.

42

Now we have to bring them down to the troposphere with a good selection of competencies, and then anchor them in specific transformation projects. Which transformation competencies do you think could help you most right now?

—I had considered these four: Project design, because it would help me in the development of a new consultative sales model; Feedback, because my team needs it and, very often, my way of providing feedback doesn't produce the impact I want; Written skills, so that my mentor doesn't suffer heart attacks from my misspelling.

—If it isn't for the right reason, it won't work.

—Calm down, calm down, I was joking. And also Matrix Influence because, although I think I'm good at it, it's essential to navigate in a complex organisation. What do you think?

—Let's begin with the last one. I wouldn't recommend you start with Matrix Influence, which in large part you in fact acquire as you acquire the other eleven transformation competencies. Let me explain. What would your influence be on people from other areas of the organisation, or from other countries, when you interact with them, if they value the fact that your diagnoses are accurate and that you contribute to designing well the project on which you are working together and that you execute with agility; if they perceive your integrity; if your closeness with them comes from a genuine interest in each person; if you give them the gift of feedback independently of levels in the hierarchy; if the observe that you communicate concisely and clearly, adding value in different formats; if you are an advanced user of digital tools in order to collaborate with them; if you handle meetings in which you participate with a disciplined methodology that facilitates the generation of collective intelligence?

—More than good, perfect, I'd say.

—By the way, I am surprised that in this competence you have given yourself such an extraordinary grade. It's very unlikely that you would reach that level with the moderate degree of development you seem to have in the other competencies.

—I'm not keen to lower my grade in one of the competencies that I think I have best developed. But I think I am beginning to perceive your style and I'm aware that you are going to say: "Self-criticism is more stimulating than self-complacency."

—Good, you can grade your intuition with an «excellent». Let's look at the other three. The competency of Project design is appropriate due to your current responsibility. But I would suggest that you replace it with the competency of Diagnosis & Decision, for two reasons. Since you live so hurriedly and it seems and you don't have much time to think and, at the same time, your Influence personality makes you somewhat hyperactive, I think that right now, to gain in seniority, it would be more useful for you to learn to develop a more systemic and structured way of thinking.

—And how do you do that?

—Tomorrow I will send you some recommended reading with which you can start to work on the competency of Diagnosis & Decision. Let's see the other two that you have selected.

—Feedback and Written skills.

—From what you say, it seems that your feedback does not produce the impact you want, perhaps because you are too direct and, sometimes, you may hurt people by the way you say things. Don't you think that you could begin by working on the competency of Closeness – hey, with Helen too – so that gain the level of confidence that is necessary for others to allow you to provide them – to put in that way - with a more transformational feedback?

—It makes sense, although I think I'm reasonably good at Closeness. After all, I spend my time travelling to countries.

—In that case let's return to your development challenges, to ensure that the competencies that you select are consistent with them.

—To cultivate a transformational leadership and advance in self discipline.

—Correct. We have now the competency of Diagnosis & Decision, which will help you to achieve a more systemic manner of thinking and, therefore, improve your intellectual discipline; and the competency of Closeness, that will help you to foster a more transformational leadership, since it is the entrance door to feedback. What do you say if we review your first reflections about the book 7 Habits? You said something about your entry tray ...

—Let me look at the platform. I remember what I wrote was from Copenhagen, so it must have been around 10th or 11th March. Here it is! «Keep my entry tray up to date, without the need to stay every night to answer unattended messages».

—Exactly. Which competency do you think will address that challenge?

—Digital Tools?

—Well now we have the three competencies to work on during the mentoring programme: Diagnosis & Decision, Closeness and Digital Tools.

—Sounds OK. I like them. But what about the other nine? Do I just forget about them?

—Don't worry. Competencies are like cherries: when you pick one, three or four come with it.

—Fantastic. Then I'll go after those three.

—Yes, but I would suggest that you begin with only one during the next ninety days. Specifically, with Closeness.

—Alright.

—Sarah, it's time to end. I would propose the following milestones for the next few weeks. In the first week, design and publish a personal transformation project with regard to the competency of Closeness, using a template I will let you have tomorrow through the platform. In weeks two and three, publish the results of your implementation of this project. And in week four, we will comment on how our videoconference went.

—Oliver, that's really cool! I promise I will give my best.

—That's great to hear. I hope everything goes well in London and that you can rest over the weekend in Copenhagen.
—Thank you very much. Ciao.

26th March | Punta del Este | 10:00
Text message published on the platform

Good morning, Sarah,

In order to keep record on the platform, I remind you of what we agreed on yesterday:

Development challenges:

- Cultivate a transformational leadership.
- Advance in self-discipline.

Competencies selected:

- Diagnosis & Decision.
- Closeness.
- Digital Tools.

I offer you some recommended reading to deepen your knowledge of these competencies. And also to cultivate your self-discipline:

Diagnosis & Decision:

- *Thinking, Fast and slow*. Daniel Kahneman
- *Are You Ready to Decide?* McKinsey Quarterly
- *How to Make your Company Smarter: Decision Making*. MITSloan Management Review

Closeness:

- *Man's Search for Meaning.* Viktor E. Frankl
- *The Speed of Trust.* Stephen R. Covey
- *Nicomachean Ethics.* Aristotle
- *Empathy.* HBR Press
- *Mindsight.* Daniel J Siegel

Digital Tools:

- *Leading Virtual Teams.* HBR Press
- *Virtual Collaboration.* HBR Press
- *The Digital Transformation.* David L. Rogers
- *How Social Tools Can Reshape the Organization.* Digital McKinsey

Discipline:

- *The Power of Habit.* Charles Duhigg
- *Focus.* Cal Newport
- *Getting Work Done.* HBR Press
- *Managing Time.* HBR Press
- *Unbeatable Mind.* Mark Divine

I attach the template that will enable you to design a personal transformation project around a competency, with an example of how to bring it down to earth. It can be applied to our transformation competencies or to any competency you might want to develop, whether it is drawn from the set of competencies proposed by the company you currently work for or from a different set that is useful to you.

Let me to emphasise one point: it is critical to learn to incorporate competencies rapidly. There is no need to confide in one single model, whether it's ours, from your current company, or from the next company in which you might work. Competency models should be to serve your needs and not the other way round.

DANIELA | VERBAL & NON-VERBAL SKILLS

SELF DIAGNOSIS 1   Scale: 4 Excellent – 3 Good – 2 Fair – 1 Bad

PROBLEM/OPPORTUNITY

I have difficulty in expressing clearly and concisely what I think. I tend to ramble, to be needlessly long winded and cause more confusion than clarity. I notice that others reduce their level of attention when I speak and, as a result, I think that by shortcomings in this competency limit my capacity to influence others.

GENERAL OBJECTIVE

Improve my influence with my team —and also in the rest of the organisation— through concise, clear communication that adds value.

SPECIFIC OBJECTIVES

- Reach an average of 3 in Concision, Clarity and Value (scale 4-3-2-1) in feedback that I will request after my participation at meetings.
- Prepare and give 6 short TED talks to my team, for the purpose of accelerating the development of the competency.

TIME FRAME: 90 days

IMPLEMENTATION

LEARNING RESOURCES

- **On Communication.** HBR's 10 Must Reads
- **Failure to Communicate.** Holly Weeks
- **Successful Writing and Speaking.** HBR Press
- **Brilliant Presentation.** Richard Hall
- **Playlist TED:** Before Public Speaking…
  https://www.ted.com/playlists/226/before_public_speaking
- **Udemy Course:** Enhance Your Speaking Voice
  https://www.udemy.com/enhance-your-speaking-voice/

DAILY

- **Evernote notebook.** Notes to organise my thoughts before talking at meetings.
- **Feedback after meetings.** At the beginning of each meeting I will explain that I am working on this competency and will ask for feedback (Scale 4-3-2-1) with regard to the Concision; the Clarity and the Value of my participation.
- **Hourglass (of 3 minutes).** I will take it to each meeting to measure the time during which I talk. I will record the total time of my participation in each meeting.
- **Telling tales:** Each night I will tell a tale to my children, trying to modulate my voice in accordance with the techniques I am studying.

WEEKLY

- **Mini TEDs.** I will start each weekly meeting with my team by giving a 5 minute TED style talk, explaining a concept that I have learned.
- **Study time:** Block two hours a week in my agenda in order to study. At the weekend, I will substitute Netflix (2 hours) for videos on communication in YouTube and in TED.

I will give you some hints to design the project:

- Make a very incisive diagnosis of the **Problem/Opportunity**.
- Define a **General Objective** that pursues the strategy of the competency, trying to respond to the development challenges the person faces.
- Define **Specific Objectives** that are sufficiently specific to be able to evaluate their progress from week to week.
- Establish a **Time Frame** for the project of sixty or ninety days. If it is necessary to extend it, successive periods of thirty days may be added.
- Specify several daily and weekly mechanisms of **Implementation**, linked to your personal and professional daily activity.
- And, as part of the implementation, work out an ambitious and demanding study plan. Your **Learning Resources** can include books, articles, podcasts, videos, etc.

Please do not hesitate to get in touch with me should you have any queries.

Oliver

28th March | Copenhagen | 08:31
Audio message published on the platform

Good morning, Oliver. I'm not sending you this message because I have any doubts about the format to design the project, which seemed very clear to me, but because, for several days, I have been brooding over what you said to me about reaching my maximum level of «juniority». Perhaps you have made a rush judgement... I don't know, maybe it's my fault for not describing my professional career in detail. I didn't graduate yesterday. It was a decade ago and from the Tec of Monterrey, which was a fantastic experience, where I learned a great deal and made a pile of friends and, the following year, I did my MBA at IE Business School, where I also learned an awful lot and I fell in love with Madrid and also, as you know, with Bryan. Anyway, before finishing the MBA I had an offer from the company where I now work, but at first they sent me for almost a year's training to a corporate university we have in Florida before bringing me to the corporate offices in Boston where I started as an analyst. Then I was promoted to coordinator. I won acknowledgements on several occasions for my management capacity. I moved through several other job assignments and, for the last two years, I have been commercial manager. Since then, I have doubled the sales of the company, although perhaps such trivial financial data doesn't impress you much. I think I told you that, in addition, I have been through programmes at Harvard and Kellogg. What else? Two years ago, I participated in a programme run by the Center for Creative Leadership and now I recall that last year I did a course at Singularity University too. I suppose that all this doesn't mean much for a veteran like you. Yes, I have read about your international career in LinkedIn and it's super cool. And by the way, I would like you to tell me your story someday, since I have practically told you all my life. Well, almost all of it. Anyhow, when I think about «juniority», to be honest, I don't see my career very different from those who are on the executive committee of our company, although they are a bit older. Well, if you compare me with our CEO... he's only thirty-nine, I think. Mind you, he's a genius. When he was twenty-eight, he founded a company which we later acquired and around three years ago the Board of Directors had the courage to put him at the head of the whole company. But when I have contact with him, the truth is that it's like talking to a friend, because Claus is quite informal. He is Danish and very practical, very uncomplicated, and he dresses casually, but with style. We will coincide in Copenhagen this week, by the way, in a meeting that is critical for my project. And Helen is coming too! Oh my

50

God! I'll let you know how it goes. Well O.K., I'm going to take a bicycle ride around Copenhagen. It's cold, but today it's been sunny. Ciao.

28th March | Copenhagen | 21:31
Audio message published on the platform

Hi, Oliver. This morning I forgot to tell you that I had downloaded Audible and that I have finished *The 7 Habits*. To be honest, both the book and the listening experience have been fascinating. I finished it this morning, in fact, while riding my bike in the centre of Copenhagen. Anyway, if I had to summarise, which I imagine you'd appreciate, the most important lesson for me from the book, I'd say that it's... it's that I have realised that I haven't spent enough time thinking about my purpose in life, or to put it in another way, in the last ten years I have lived exclusively for my professional ambition. And we can say that it hasn't gone badly, but not in all ways. In fact, my relationship with Bryan hasn't been so good lately. I know that this mentoring is professional but, I don't know, I think your perspective and your experience could help me with this subject. Well, there's time for us to talk about this. Ciao.

(...)

Wait, I forgot, which is the next book like *The 7 Habits* that you would recommend me? Thank you.

(...)

Ah, something else! To reflect about my purpose in life, it would be good for me to know how to formulate it. I know it's me who's doing the mentoring programme, not you. But forgive me if I ask you a bold question: could you tell me your purpose in life? Ciao.

Text message published on the platform

Good morning, Sarah,

I have just listened to the messages that you sent to me on Saturday.

I can see that you have been educated at first class educational institutions, but people do not transform themselves by attending courses, doing programmes or obtaining certificates, like collecting stamps in a passport. That, alone, is academic tourism. Rather, people are transformed through *learning by doing*, from the daily exercise of the will, by developing the good habits and building the character that are required for assuming the responsibilities of leadership. It's from there, from the character, that leaders really lead. The hierarchy, by itself, simply issues instructions that are carried out in direct proportion to the existence of control mechanisms of reward and retribution. This explains why so much lack of leadership comes to the surface in senior managers whose companies pay endlessly to provide them with the experience of first-class academic tourism. But «travelling» alone, without a leader who uses a healthy combination of discipline and closeness to accompany them in their development process. And this is precisely the loneliness that is experienced by so many people whose bosses are only managers orientated to operations and who delegate the development of their teams to human resources departments.

With regard to the concept of «juniority»—although it would appear to be counterintuitive—it doesn't cure itself with the passage of time, but with self-development. Although, whilst you are working on it, there is no reason to be concerned.

I am very glad to hear that you have finished reading the first book. Your reflections are quite deep and acute. Rather than a book on management, now I prefer to recommend you a biography that might interest you, since you like tennis: *Open*, by Andre Agassi.

On the subject of my purpose in life, I discovered it on the way to Barajas airport in Madrid, more than ten years ago. Although I really understood it better on my return.

For two years, I had to travel frequently to the capital of Spain to provide follow-up for a transformation programme of a well-known company. In this context, a natural harmony arose with a manager with whom I had spent many hours in conversation on professional subjects, almost always in the presence of other people. One day he offered to take me to the airport, and, on the way, he suddenly opened the door of his private life and led me «into the kitchen». He had been separated from his wife for two years. He was frustrated because he lived alone and only saw his son, Jaime, just five years old, when it was his turn, in accordance with the terms of the divorce settlement. He had envisioned something different for his life. He had studied at the University of Navarre and had then done an MBA at London Business School. His career in his organisation was promising, he had big ambitions and a lot of plans, but they all froze after the separation, as if an arctic cold had suddenly hit his life. He said that he felt like a wounded animal: dejected, evasive, and aggressive; sometimes all at the same time, and at other times, one by one. He was empty, without that interior strength that had moved him all his life. I listened to him with attention and I suggested that he might like to read *Wild at Heart*, a book written by John Eldredge which had helped me better to understand how a man's heart works. I told him that Eldredge maintains that there are three forces that energise a man's life: «an adventure to live, a battle to fight and beauty to rescue». Or to re-rescue, I added, surprised that I had been so forthright: «Why don't you go and see your wife and propose that you come back together again», I said, entertaining the somewhat remote prospect that he would do so. When we reached the airport, he thanked me and gave me a hug, adding a terse: «Have a good trip». To which I replied unwittingly: «You too».

Two months later, when I had to return to Madrid, he wrote to me and offered to pick me up at the airport. I insisted that it was better for me to take a taxi because my plane arrived after 11 o'clock at night. I was unable to dissuade him. When I reached the gate that separates passengers from chauffeurs, family and friends, there was Felipe waiting for me, holding Jaime on one arm, both of them with a countenance that reflected an Olympic joy. We got into the car and as soon as Jaime went to sleep, he said to me: «We are together again». To my surprise, he told me that the day we had had that conversation, that very day, he bought the book and went to see his wife. A short time later, they returned to living together. And a few months later, he announced that Jaime was going to have a brother. The day that that creature appeared for the first time in my Facebook Timeline, my purpose in life was overturned. Until that date it was to contribute to the transformation of organisations. But that day I understood that the most promising way of achieving it was the transformation of people. Of each person. And my work then, and now, is a magnificent platform for this purpose.

I trust that the meeting with Claus and with Helen will go well. I look forward to receiving your project so that I can provide you with feedback.

Oliver

Oliver, I am writing from the Wi-Fi of an aircraft returning to Boston. I don't know where to begin... These days in Copenhagen have been strange.

On Sunday afternoon I met Claus in the hotel, and he invited me to dinner. He was there to spend the weekend with his parents in Aarhus, a city located on the east coast of the Jutland peninsula. As always, he was very spontaneous and very agreeable. He even told me about his family and his childhood in Aarhus. Everything was fine until he mentioned Helen... He said that he has decided to have her close by to keep a record of his meetings and to have an updated balanced scorecard available on the status of everything. He even said that he is like Lennon, an irreverent visionary, and that he needs someone at his side like McCartney, congenial and disciplined. Helen McCartney... All that I needed! Fortunately, she reached the hotel too late to join us at dinner.

The meeting on Monday was a disaster... What happened was that the complicity between Claus and Helen began to irritate me from the beginning of the meeting. And when it was my turn to present the results of the first quarter, after the third figure that Helen questioned, I explained that it was me who had the final figures of all the countries because I was in permanent personal contact with them, not sitting comfortably in my office in the corporate office... She said that her information was the information provided by the countries, with which she had direct access. In short, we became embroiled in an absurd conversation and Claus had to cut us off sharply to request that we move on to the next point on the agenda because we were running short of time. You should have seen the «gaze of projection» I threw at Helen... I'm beginning to think that someone in my team is selling me out, passing information to

Helen...

Afterwards, I sent her a coded *whatsapp*... Here is a copy, you see what you think:

> «Helen...
> from now on...
> if you are going to present data at a meeting...
> I would appreciate that you check them out with me in advance...
> it's easy to play out of tune when you haven't got the right music sheet...
> so you'd better *#letitbe*»

Several hours later, she sent me a loooooong email, with a copy to Claus, which I will not bore you with, because it was a series of clarifications and refinements of our discussion during the meeting, which, by the way, completely ignored the context of the information I tried to present in spite of her interruptions... I had to reply, point by point, with a copy to Claus. Exhausting... This is the part of my job that I detest, company politics...

Moving to another subject, I have asked my team to give me their diagnosis of how they see me in respect of the competency of closeness. I will wait for the results and on Friday and I will upload the project.

I don't want to forget to say that what you told me about your purpose in life was touching... I like this Oliver more than the one I met halfway through February...

I still have another five hours of flying. I will start with *Open*. I'll tell you what I think.

Sarah

Hi, Oliver. Let me tell you that on Friday I received feedback from my team about my degree of development of the competency Closeness. I confess that it left me so mentally blocked that until today I wasn't in the mood to do the project. I have received some surprises. Above all, with Monika, the person in my team who is in Berlin. She was very hard on me. I enumerate some of the opportunities for me to improve that they have identified, although they don't all share the same opinion. I'll read them to you: «She doesn't have a genuine interest in others. She lacks empathy and capacity to listen. She is impatient to impose her own agenda. She isn't worried or doesn't think about the impact she has on others. And in the face of conflict, or an attack, or criticism, she becomes mentally blocked». But what most surprised me was Monika's final note: «I welcome this initiative of asking us for our opinion about your leadership. It would be extraordinary if you also extended it to the work we do». I don't understand why she is accusing me of not asking for her opinion about work, when in my team we are all in permanent contact through WhatsApp and they know they can say whatever they like, whenever they like. Anyway... Precisely next week I will be talking to Monika. I have to go to Berlin. I don't feel like it at all, but that's the way it is. I attach the project on Closeness. I look forward to your feedback. Ciao.

SARAH | CLOSENESS

SELF DIAGNOSIS 1   Scale: 4 Excellent – 3 Good – 2 Fair – 1 Bad

PROBLEM/OPPORTUNITY

I have always considered myself personally close to my team, in spite of the fact that at times I am perceived as abrupt, too direct and too work-focused. The recent feedback from several people in my team, however, has left me thinking that I have a significant opportunity for improvement: «She isn't genuinely interested in others.» «She lacks empathy and capacity to listen.» «She is impatient to impose her own agenda.» «She isn't worried or doesn't think about the effect she has on others.» «Any conflict, attack, or criticism blocks her up.» Am I close with some and distant with others?

GENERAL OBJECTIVE

Recover the trust of the people in my team who see me as distant in order to achieve greater alignment in the implementation of our project.

SPECIFIC OBJECTIVES

- Foster trust with all the people in my team.
- At meetings, listen more and be less impulsive.

TIME FRAME: 90 days

IMPLEMENTATION

LEARNING RESOURCES

- *Man's Search for Meaning*, Viktor E. Frankl
- *The Speed of Trust*, Steven Covey
- *Nicomachean Ethics*, Aristotle
- *Empathy*, HBR Press
- *Mindsight*, Daniel J Siegel

These are what you sent me. I don't know where to begin. Any suggestion?

DAILY

- Listen more.
- Don't interrupt at meetings.
- Substitute some emails or messages with phone calls.
- Leave room in my agenda to have conversations of a non-professional nature with the members of my team with whom I do not have an easy relationship.

WEEKLY

- Make a phone call each week to each member of my team.
- When I am travelling, have lunch with the local team.

58

Text message published on the platform

Good morning, Sarah,

I trust that you have been able to rest from your trip to Copenhagen. With regard to the project for the competency Closeness, my comments are as follows:

- The Diagnosis of the Problem/Opportunity is valid. And to ask for feedback would certainly appear to be a good way to discover our blind spot, that which we don't see about ourselves. Maybe it could be summed up by saying that you have a «selective closeness» and that you orientate it towards those people you get on well with, a category to which Monika would not appear to belong.
- You have given the General Objective too much of a tactical orientation: «Achieve greater alignment in the implementation of our project». It isn't a bad aim in itself, but it's too small for you and too confined to a specific time frame. What about formulating the General Objective as follows?: «Recover the trust of the people in my team who see me as distant, in order to develop a more flexible and adaptable leadership, learning to empathize with diverse personalities».
- The Specific Objectives are not sufficiently specific to be able to measure your progress week by week. Try to use an explicit indicator of your progress in the development of trust with the members of your team. What about measuring the degree of trust with each one of them and reviewing it every week? For example, on a scale from 1 to 10, with Monika it seems that you must be around 1 or 2, because, as you said, next week you have to go to Berlin, and you don't «feel like it at all». And then, with regard to the objective «listen more and be less impulsive at meetings», how about taking to some

59

meetings a card with the definition of the type of listening you want to achieve and at the end of the meeting asking the participants for a quick evaluation by noting on the card their perception from 1 to 4 (1 Bad – 2 Average – 3 Good – 4 Excellent)?

- With regard to Learning Resources, I suggest that you begin with Man's Search for Meaning by Viktor E. Frankl. It doesn't deal directly with the competency Closeness, but it gives you food for thought about it. This is what the outline from Amazon says: «A prominent Viennese psychiatrist before the war, Viktor Frankl, was uniquely able to observe the way that both he and others in Auschwitz coped (or didn't) with the experience. He noticed that it was the men who comforted others and who gave away their last piece of bread who survived the longest—and who offered proof that everything can be taken away from us except the ability to choose our attitude in any given set of circumstances». I read this book when I started at university. I remember that it was a Sunday afternoon. I drank it down in one. Over the years I have returned several times to that afternoon, when I have had to meet suffering face to face.

- In the Implementation section, I would suggest that you note in your diary a brief period of time every day when you will evaluate your progress in the specific practices of Closeness that you have chosen to carry out, and another period of time each week. I put forward some other practices, should they be of any use to you: make a note of what you know about the life of each person in your team and of your peers in the organisation (professional career, family, hobbies, birthdays, etc.) and also of their development opportunities (how they come out in the DISC, which leadership challenges their personality present, what feedback you have given or would like to give them, etc.) and have lunch every day with a person with whom you need to gain in closeness. If you see that any of these practices doesn't work, at any time you can take them off the list. And if a new one occurs to you, you update the project. It should be a flexible and practical instrument. Where you have to be inflexible is in your discipline in implementing it.

Sarah, may I suggest that you publish on the platform the updated project and that you publish as well your most significant achievements this week.

On the other hand, I would like to make a suggestion of style. Moderate your use of ellipses. This is too informal in a professional context. An another about the use of WhatsApp: when you write a message—such as the one you sent to Helen— if you compose the complete text and send it once, you deliver just one notification to the other person, instead of interrupting the receiver several times. Attention to detail is a sign of respect for the other person. By the way, it is difficult to perceive respect in the message you sent to Helen. Moreover, sending ironic messages to let off steam emotionally usually has unwanted consequences that are unforeseeable.

In order to prepare your encounter with Monika in Berlin, I would recommend that you watch the TED talk 5 Ways to Listen Better and a video on YouTube called How to Really Listen to People.

Oliver

Text message published on the platform

Hi, Oliver.

This morning I had thought of sending you an audio message, but I preferred to do so now in writing so that you can see that I have moderated my use of dots.

I attach the second version of the project for the competency Closeness, in which I have taken into account your recommendations. I have a query. Aren't they too many points in which to improve? Wouldn't it be better to focus on one or two things and add others progressively?

I am also sending my achievements of this week:

- I watched the two videos you recommended and—although I didn't in the least feel like it—I forced myself to have a conversation with Monika. I suggested that we should have lunch together and she accepted, but with a gesture of resignation, as if to keep her distance. I told her that I wanted to understand her feedback and, surprisingly, the conversation was fluid. I applied the technique I learned in one of the videos: «Receive, appreciate, summarise and ask». If you had seen me, you wouldn't have recognised me. I let her talk practically without interruption and, at the end, I assured her that I would think about what she told me, and I thanked her. I told her that I was doing an online mentoring programme and that I was going to incorporate her recommendations into the project to work on the competency of Closeness and it fascinated her. She asked me to pass on to her the information about the programme. So, if an application arrives from a certain Monika, you know who recommended her... (And I'm not going to remove those dots).

SARAH | CLOSENESS VERSION 2

SELF DIAGNOSIS 1   Scale: 4 Excellent – 3 Good – 2 Fair – 1 Bad

PROBLEM/OPPORTUNITY

I have always considered myself personally close to my team, in spite of the fact that at times I am perceived as abrupt, too direct and too work-focused. The recent feedback from several people in my team, however, has left me thinking that I have a significant opportunity for improvement: «She isn't genuinely interested in others.» «She lacks empathy and capacity to listen.» «She is impatient to impose her own agenda.» «She isn't worried or doesn't think about the effect she has on others.» «Any conflict, attack, or criticism blocks her up.» In short, it seems that my «closeness» is selective.

GENERAL OBJECTIVE

Recover the trust of the people in my team who see me as distant in order to develop a more flexible and adaptable leadership, learning how to tune to different personalities.

SPECIFIC OBJECTIVES

- Foster trust with all the people in my team. **Indicator:** degree of closeness with each person (scale 1-2-3-4 /self evaluation). Achieve 3 with all of them in 90 days. Weekly review.
- At meetings, listen more and be less impulsive. **Indicator:** "Active Listening" index card (scale 1-2-3-4 / evaluation from team). Achieve an average of 3.

TIME FRAME 90 days

IMPLEMENTATION

LEARNING RESOURCES

- *Man's Search for Meaning.* Viktor E. Frankl
- *The Speed of Trust.* Stephen R. Covey
- *Nicomachean Ethics.* Aristotle
- *Empathy.* HBR Press
- *Mindsight.* Daniel J Siegel

DAILY

- Do not interrupt at meetings, ask more and listen more. Indicator: "active listening" index card (scale 1-2-3-4 / evaluation from team). Achieve an average of 3.
- Substitute an email or message with a phone call to the person I question.
- Have lunch with someone every day, not alone at my desk.
- Make notes of what I learn about each member of my team and about my peers (results of their DISC, what leadership opportunities are available due to their personality, what feedback have I given them or would like to give them, etcetera). Tool: OneNote

WEEKLY

- Make a call each week to a member of my team.
- When I am travelling, have lunch with the local team.
- Weekly review of the indicator of closeness with each person (scale 1-2-3-4 /self evaluation). Surpass 3 with all of them in 90 days.

63

- On the trip from Boston to Berlin I started reading Man's Search for Meaning. I still haven't got far enough to understand how this book is going to help me in my «selective closeness», but I am enjoying it. Agassi's book is fascinating. It's not clear to me whether you consider me as obstinate as his father or as savagely sincere like him. I finished it in three or four late nights. The good news is that I am about to cancel my subscription to Netflix. The bad news is that Habitify reminds me each day that I'm not fulfilling my resolution to sleep at least seven hours.

On another front, last week I had another exchange of very disagreeable emails with Helen. I'm thinking about going and talking to Claus this week.

Sarah

13th April | Punta del Este | 08:12
Text message published on the platform

Good morning, Sarah,

I congratulate you on your achievements of last week. Most particularly, for the conversation with Monika. Learning to listen isn't easy, particularly for personalities with Dominance traits, such as impatience and self-sufficiency. But it's one of those efforts from which you quickly reap the benefit. It helps to get to know the other person better and what he or she really thinks. Not necessarily to reach an immediate agreement on everything but certainly to widen our perspective on our surrounding reality and to be able to build on a common ground, although it sometimes may seem very small.

The Closeness project is now well anchored. It's true that the points you have selected for implementation are ambitious, but they are also attainable. And moreover, they are not «extra work», you can incorporate them naturally into your daily activity within your current agenda.

According to your message, you read Agassi's book in three or four late night sessions and, at the same time, Habitify is reminding you that you are not meeting your commitment to sleep at least seven hours a day. It is critical that you re-adjust the priorities in your diary to avoid tension between your different challenges. Perhaps it would be an appropriate moment for you to review how you orchestrate the work with your team by reading *Delegating Work*, a very short book—but very practical—published by HBR press.

With regard to the open conflict with Helen and the conversation you wish to have with Claus, I would suggest that you postpone it. I would like to be able to understand better how your relationship is transpiring so that I can offer you some ideas about how to deal with it. On this issue, I would pose you two questions in anticipation of our next videoconference (planned for 28th April): Which virtues does Helen have? What does she do well?

Oliver

20th April | Punta del Este | 08:04
Text message published on the platform

Good morning, Sarah,

Last week you didn't publish any achievement. Is everything alright?

Oliver

Oliver, I must tell you something that happened to me yesterday. Guess who it's about: our friend Helen. In short, I put my foot in it. I'll explain. Claus called me to his office to ask me about the status of the proposal we sent to a possible new client in London. It's a great opportunity. And what's more, I think we're going to get the order! I think I said something about this before. Anyway, we started going into details and there was Helen taking notes of what we were saying, like McCartney at the piano. At a certain point, Helen mentioned the contents of an email that I sent to the client, with a copy to part of my team, but not to her. I immediately jumped at her throat: «And what's this? Espionage?» So Helen goes and says: «No, it's called collaboration and teamwork», with that tone that gets on my nerves. If it weren't for an incoming call to Claus at that precise moment, I could have strangled her there and then, in the chairman's office. But this wasn't the blunder, no, no, the blunder was the *whatsapp* I sent to my friend Andrea when I left the meeting. Just a moment. Let me send you a copy, and then I'll finish the story.

> «Andre, you aren't going to believe it!!!!!!!
> McCartney has found the way of reading my emails!!
> one day she'll have to explain what she has done to have access to EVERYTHING...
> and above all, to what doesn't concern her...
> her longing to control has no limits...
> this woman needs *#help*»

OK, I know the message breaks all the rules of grammar and style that you have been passing on to me for the last two months and won't help me to get out of my «juniority», but at least acknowledge that it's not easy to contain yourself with such a person... Anyway. I got it wrong and instead of sending the text to Andrea I sent it to Helen herself!!! *Oof...* now it's me that needs *#help*... Well, to finish painting the picture, let me tell you that Helen replied to my message and what she said has left me quite apprehensive. Here it is:

> «Sarah, I was surprised to receive your message but not by the contents. They portray you. I suggest you concentrate on achieving results and complying with the professional standards of the company. Don't worry about me, *#Ifeelfine*»

Any suggestion to get out of this mess?

Sara

24th April | Punta del Este | 09:09
Text message published on the platform

Good Morning, Sarah,

To answer your question, I have a long and a short answer. The long answer is a maxim: «If you find yourself in a hole, stop digging». And the short one is: disconnect and get some rest.

We'll talk next week.

Oliver

27th April | London | 21:02
Text message published on the platform

Good evening, Oliver,

Just arrived in London. In preparation for our conversation tomorrow, I send you my *#achievements* of these last two weeks, when I have been missing.

- I grasp the essence of the maxim, but I need your

refinements. Furthermore, I heeded your «short answer». On Saturday, I slept eleven hours in a row. I was exhausted. I don't know whether this counts as an #achievement but at least it improves my statistics with Habitify.

- I have been out running three times in two weeks. Well below my objective but raising the average.
- I have advanced very little with Man's Search for Meaning. That's because a Netflix series has trapped me. Tidying up with Marie Kondo! No, it isn't the typical action series with violence and superficial human relationships. It's something that, in fact, is helping me to put my house in order. Bryan still doesn't believe it...
- Right away tomorrow, I'm going to start implementing my «active listening» card. My friend Andrea designed it for me last weekend, following the suggestions you gave me. I have decided to use it in five meetings per week. What do you think of it?

I am participating in a mentoring programme in which I am working on the competency called Closeness, through **ACTIVE LISTENING**, which is defined as:

Showing genuine interest in what the other person wants to say, listening with the eyes, not interrupting, and summing up to validate.

HOW WOULD YOU EVALUATE ME DURING THIS MEETING?
Scale: 4 Excellent – 3 Good – 2 Fair – 1 Bad

DATE					
GRADE					

—Hullo Sarah, how are you?

—Fine, thanks, and you?

—Very well. And how do you feel about your self-development achievements in the last month?

—I feel good about them, to be honest. Although not entirely satisfied.

—We have several subjects of conversation for today.

—Right. What about starting by you explaining what you meant with the maxim «if you find yourself in a hole, stop digging». It's been running through my head all the weekend. Andrea has her own interpretation, but I prefer to hear yours.

—The hole is the relationship you have with Helen. And every heated message you send to her is another spadeful.

—That's what I was afraid of.

—Why?

—Just what Andrea said to me.

—In that case, let's continue. I would recommend you move on to some new reading for your learning resources: Nichomachean Ethics, by Aristotle. I think that, particularly now, it would be good for you to think about what this wise man says about prudence.

—Can you give me an advance?

—According to Aristotle, a prudent person is one who knows how to deliberate without orientating the will towards immediate pleasure but towards good, towards that which leads to lasting happiness both to oneself and to others.

—And what's that got to do with Helen?

—Rather than with Helen, it has to do with the relationship that you are maintaining with her. I think that if you reflect on the virtue of prudence, it will help you to identify what you are aiming at, deep down, with those messages that you send her, what impact they may have on her and what are you expecting from your professional relationship.

—More than philosophy, what I like is action. But I take up the glove.

—Have you thought about the two questions I asked you about Helen: which virtues does she have and what does she do well?

—Around about... ten seconds.

—In that case, if you are in agreement, we'll leave that task for next week and you can give me your conclusions.

—O.K. Oliver, but I want you to understand that with the pressure for results, with all the travelling I endure, I need a fast response to any obstacle between me and my objectives. Understand?

—...

—And that crazy woman is a real obstacle. Or have you never let the wrong word escape or a message you regretted?

—Calm down. Breathe deeply. Three times.

—O.K.

—Yes, Sarah. I also released messages I regretted. Enough of them to learn that it is better to choose your battles with care and fight them at the right moment.

—What do you mean by choose your battles?

—Some time ago, my friend Daniel told me that his seven-year-old son had insulted his wife, Martha, while they were having breakfast. Immediately, and firmly, he told him to be quiet and he changed the subject. That same afternoon, he told his son that he wanted to talk with him. They went out on to the porch of their house, sat on the steps and Daniel spoke to him in the following terms: «I met Martha twelve years ago. I thought she was the most beautiful woman in the world. I fell in love with her gentleness, her generosity, her way of looking after small things. So, I asked her to marry me and, incredibly, she accepted me, and we decided to share the rest of our lives. On this journey, your brother Paul soon joined us. Later, you arrived too and, only three years ago, your sister Olivia. It's true that over these years we have had some hard times... I suppose like any other married couple. But we have been very happy. I feel very fortunate to be Martha's husband. My friends still can't understand how I managed to captivate the most beautiful girl at the university. I love her with all my heart, and I would do anything that may be necessary to protect our marriage. And to protect her. And so, if anyone ever tried to hurt her, if anyone dared to do her harm or insult her, they would find themselves up against me. And that includes you. Don't ever speak to Martha again like you did this morning at breakfast. Is that clear? Instead, treat her with all the love you can muster. You are never going to find a better mother. In all the world...».

—...

—Are you alright, Sarah?

—Yes... It's just that... You have reminded me of my mother.

—It's okay.

—Go on...

—Take your time.

—Forgive me... Go on, go on.

—I'm sorry. It wasn't my intention to make you cry or to remind you of your mother.

—Well you've done both. And my mother is a subject I'm not prepared to broach.

—My intention was to illustrate the importance of choosing which battles to fight and when.

— Yes, I know.

—With regard to Helen, it's obvious that you need to talk to restore your relationship. You have every right to be frustrated by her behaviour, although I would doubt if your motives are always reasonable and proportionate. But it would be better to look for—or rather, find—the right moment to have a conversation. Instead of sending poisonous messages or over-reacting when she says or does something that irritates you. Even less in public.

—I think you'd get on well with Andrea. It's as though you

71

agree to see things from a different angle. But anyway, I'll think about it.

—I'm glad to coincide with your friend, as long as that helps you. Let's move on. You said before that you were not altogether satisfied with your self-development achievements in the last month. Why?

—Because I haven't achieved what I proposed to achieve. In fact, I've achieved practically nothing. What do you think? How do you see me?

—You advance inconsistently, making last moment sprints.

—I have always been one of those who studies the night before the exam.

—And I imagine that part of the problem is that, in addition, you obtained good grades.

—Yes. Well, not always. But in general, things went well for me at school and at university. And why do you think that's a problem?

—Because your memory—and, perhaps, your mental agility—have allowed you to obtain good academic results and perhaps professional results as well, in spite of not being, let's say, a model of discipline.

—Not a good model. No.

—Which brings us to a subject that we postponed during our last videoconference.

—Yes, I know: head, heart and hands.

—That's right.

—Let's start with the head. I'm all ears.

—For you, as a leader, how important is feedback?

—Absolutely.

—And in the last thirty days, how often have you given feedback to your peers or to your team?

—Do WhatsApp messages count?

—They don't.

—In that case, once or no times, depending on whether you consider that the conversation I had with Monika counts.

—Rather than giving feedback, you received it, didn't you?

—OK. In that case the answer is "zero times". But I have a doubt: when I have to evaluate my team each year, would that count?

—It doesn't count very much. Frequently, it is a purely hierarchical format and designed for a utilitarian purpose, that is to say, for bosses to justify to their teams the decisions they have taken about the annual bonuses they will receive. At other times, it is a process designed by human resources so that, at least once a year, bosses talk to their teams about their professional development and not just about business and operations.

—Now that you say that, I don't know which of the two for me is more artificial, when they evaluate me or when I have to evaluate my team.

—I think that adjective defines the process very well. Although I'm not saying that I think it's unnecessary. But genuine feedback, for me, is something else.

—What is genuine feedback for you?

—In the business environment, feedback is a gift that any person in the organisation, independently of hierarchy, can give to any other, when, instead of criticising under your breath or behind people's backs, you present a person with an opportunity to improve and you offer to help, trusting in that person's capacity for transformation.

—It sounds good.

—By the way, if I remember rightly, a couple of years ago you did a leadership programme at the Center for Creative Leadership. Possibly one of the best programmes in the world to enhance feedback as a competency.

—That's right.

—Did you like it?

—I thought it was fantastic. Amongst many other things, I learned a very practical technique for giving feedback. It's called SBI (Situation Behaviour Impact). You outline the situation in which something happened, you indicate what the behaviour was, and you explain the impact it had from your perspective. Do you know it?

—Yes, I do. And you, personally, how did you come out of the programme?

—Enthusiastic. In fact, I passed on all the documentation to my team and I made the resolution to provide feedback every week, both professional and personal.

—A good resolution, I would say, but your objective remained too generic. Did you fulfil it?

—At the beginning, yes. Especially with Bryan. But after a few days he asked me to lower the volume of intensity. I really had the poor man tormented.

—For how many weeks did you keep it up?

—One and a half. Maybe two.

—Let's sum up. I imagine that you agree that there is no more transformational a tool than a face to face conversation. And that feedback is a format that is particularly compelling.

—It would never have occurred to me to put it that way, but I agree.

—There you have it. Providing feedback appears reasonable to your head. It appears desirable to your heart. But you find it difficult to grasp it with your hands, to reduce it to concrete facts.

—Head, heart and hands. Now I do understand. And what are most difficult for me are the hands.

—For you, for Andre Agassi and for anyone.

—And to you?

—To me too.

—I'm glad to know you're a human being.

—More than you would imagine.

—I don't know. You seem impeccable to me, so sensible. Forgive me... so boring. Don't you ever give yourself a break? I mean, like breaking your diet and eating a hamburger with chips?

—Sometimes.
—Please, send me a photo the day you do, it would be so inspiring.
—Alright, I will. But would that really be inspiring for you?
—Very much so.
—Interesting. Let's go back to your development challenges.
—I do remember: cultivate a transformational leadership and gain in discipline.
—Good. At this moment of the programme, I would suggest that you work for the next month with discipline on the implementation of your project for the competency Closeness, fulfilling the daily and weekly commitments you indicated, and publishing your achievements on the platform. And if you advance sufficiently, in a month you can design the next project.
—Digital Tools.
—That's right.
—By the way, what did you think about my card for «active listening»?
—Superb. It will be a very practical instrument to measure your progress.
—Andre is the greatest.
—Sarah, it's time to end.
—I have a last question: what is an Englishman like you doing living in Punta del Este? They say it's an incredible place.
—It's a dream I had years ago with Valentina, my wife. She is Uruguayan and her family has some land down here. So, I ceased being the general manager of my company and left it in the hands of one of my partners—I only attend meetings of the Board of Directors—and now I am mainly engaged with my passion of mentoring people with high potential. Like you.
—Since when?
—We came two years ago. Although we usually spend from June to August in our home in Windsor.
—It sounds like the life of a star from Hollywood.
—There are many reasons for me to be thankful, but don't get

it wrong, in the film of my life there have also been some tragic scenes. As in anyone's. I don't know of any heart that at least some time hasn't experienced disconsolate grief.

—...
—Sarah?
—...
—I trust everything will go well for you in London.
—Thank you very much, Oliver. Today you have left me with plenty for my head. And also for my heart.
—Let's see how you grip it with your hands.
—You'll see. Ciao.

4th May | Boston | 11:50
Audio message published on the platform

Hi Oliver, you're not going to believe it. We have won the London contract! They have just notified us, and I wanted to let you know. Claus has sent a message with his congratulations to all the company. My team is overjoyed! Me too! This probably doesn't count as a self-development achievement, but you will admit that that it's a super transformational achievement. At last our new model of consultative sales is beginning to bear fruit. I'm so happy! I'll give you the details later on. Ciao.
(...)
Well, why not? Now that I think about it, of course this is an achievement for the competency Closeness. Tomorrow, in fact, I travel to London again—all the team from Europe will come—and we are going to celebrate in style. So, I hope you join the party by opening a bottle of something to toast from down there. Ciao.

4th May | Boston | 14:59
Text message published on the platform

Good afternoon, Oliver,

This morning, with the excitement of the new client, I forgot to ask a question about a subject that I have been pondering all weekend. I was going over our videoconference mentally and I was left with the impression that you didn't like the use I made of the word "inspiring". So, if you will forgive my impertinence, I would like to leave you with a task to upload onto the platform: for you, what does it mean to inspire?

Sarah

4th May | Punta del Este | 17:00
Text message published on the platform

I am delighted to hear the news, Sarah!

I join in the congratulations and tomorrow I will celebrate it with Valentina, opening perhaps more than one bottle. We'll have an asado in the garden because my daughter Claire, who lives in London, will be spending a few days with us.

I would suggest that you take advantage of the celebration of the new client to strengthen the closeness with each person in your team and to give each of them a present, but in the form of a feedback. It's enough for it to be something small and specific that helps them with their development. Try to apply the SBI technique that you learned: Situation Behaviour Impact.

With regard to the question—«what does it mean to inspire?»— I prefer to answer by explaining firstly what it does not mean to inspire. To inspire is not to occasionally dazzle someone, like a deer caught in the headlights. Because it's possible for someone to dazzle others by being quick at numbers, or by being skilled in negotiating, or by having a good eye for diagnosis, or perhaps by arousing superficial emotions in others when speaking in public. But none of this has anything to do with inspiration.

I think we live in such a superficial and such a sentimental culture that we run the risk of calling anything inspiring. Oscar Wilde expresses it evocatively: «A sentimentalist is simply one who wants to have the luxury of an emotion without paying for it». Like wanting to reach the peak of a mountain by helicopter, instead of climbing it gradually, step by step, and firstly enduring fatigue and only afterwards experiencing the joy of reaching the summit. And this tendency to obtain quick success or instantaneous satisfaction perhaps explains the rise of motivational speakers at corporate events, who are frequently invited to arouse superficial emotions in teams that do not find the lives of their bosses sufficiently inspiring.

That is why I would rather say that someone inspires you when they help you to change your habits, transforming who you are. And this is the true barometer of inspiration, your real capacity to contribute to improving the people around you. Not only making them think or arousing their emotions, but also helping them to bring things down to their hands, to the concrete facts, developing habits that form the character.

I trust my answer will be of help.

Oliver

8th May | Boston | 06:33
Text message published on the platform

Good morning, Oliver,

Now back in Boston and with the help of jet lag, I got up early this morning to tell you about my #achievements of this week, before the meetings start at the office. I think that beginning the week with the news of having gained a new client has had a stimulating effect on my self-development.

- According to Habitify, my hours of sleep have improved so little that it is insignificant. However, my reading time has improved a great deal (something more than seven hours a week), thanks mainly to Audible, which allows me «to read» every day on my way to the office and back, and also during my trips. In fact, I'm about to finish Aristotle's Nichomachean Ethics. It isn't a short book and it isn't a book to be read quickly. I think you overdid it a bit trying to make a dispersed and intense brain like mine philosophize. Although I admit that the book has some memorable pearls:

- «Prudence cannot be scientific knowledge nor art... It is a true and reasoned state of capacity to act with regard to the things that are good or bad for man». And for woman, I would add, with a more updated sensibility.

- «Wisdom is scientific knowledge combined with intuitive reason of the things that are highest in nature. On the other hand, prudence is concerned with the human good. It is not limited to what is universal but must also know the particulars, for it is practical. Prudence is generally concerned with individual matters. While young men become geometricians and mathematicians and wise in matters like these, they cannot be prudent, because prudence pertains to actions, which are necessarily particular. A young man has no experience, for it is length of time that gives experience». A deeper way of explaining your concept of «juniority», I would say.

- «Intelligence is not the same as prudence. Intelligence is concerned with the same kind of object as prudence, problems and solutions that require deliberation. But prudence goes further; it orders what should or should not be done». In other words, intelligence can tell you that it is not a good thing to stuff yourself with chocolate, but prudence suggests that it's best for you not to open the cupboard where the bar of chocolate is.

- «We know that in order to consolidate behaviour it is indispensable to repeat the same acts. This is why it is said that whoever sows acts, reaps habits, and whoever reaps habits, cultivates their own character». It's a discovery to know that when I don't open the cupboard where the chocolate is, or when I don't send that whatsapp, or when I keep my mouth shut at a meeting, I am building my character.

- «Together with biological nature, received before birth, man (and woman!) is capable of acquiring a second nature: through acts that we repeat and forget, we forge a manner of being the way we are that remains. But freedom always offers a dual and dangerous fundamental possibility. Thus, some become just and others unjust, some laborious and others lazy, responsible or irresponsible, peaceable or violent, truthful or untruthful, reflexive or reckless, constant or inconstant. Freedom thus offers us the possibility of performing good or bad acts. In the former case, we acquire virtues, in the latter, vices." What a blow... and I always thought that freedom was doing whatever I please...

- My pending task: Which virtues does Helen have? I think she is disciplined, systematic and constant. What does she do well? Excel, PowerPoint and IT in general. She's super techie. She's also good at organising, planning and following up.

- My indicator for Closeness with the people of my team is moving upwards (let me remind you that I have four direct reports and another eight across the organisation). In the first measurement (scale 1-2-3-4), the average was 2. Now we are near 3. Undoubtedly, the key has been the daily calls I have made (substituting messages or emails) and also because I have moved from having lunch alone five days a week to having lunch with a member of my team almost every day. What I haven't done is the task of making notes about what I know about each of them. I did start opening a note on OneNote on my computer, but it didn't synchronise with my cell phone and now I can't find it. I admit that I'm a disaster with technology.

- The active listening card has been a real hit. Some people have copied me. I attach the results of the four meetings at which I used it this week. I think I'm improving.

I am participating in a mentoring programme in which I am working on the competency called Closeness, through **ACTIVE LISTENING**, which is defined as:

Showing genuine interest in what the other person wants to say, listening with the eyes, not interrupting, and summing up to validate.

HOW WOULD YOU EVALUATE ME DURING THIS MEETING?
Scale: 4 Excellent – 3 Good – 2 Fair – 1 Bad

DATE	May 4th	May 5th	May 6th	May 7th		
GRADE	3	3	2	3		
	1	2	3	3		
	1	2	2	3		
	2	2	1	3		
	2	3	3	4		
	2	2	3	4		
	3	2	2	3		
		1				

As you can see, I have moved into the #HeadHeartandHands mode.

Sarah

8th May | Punta del Este | 09:09
Text message published on the platform

Good morning, Sarah,

May I congratulate you for your #achievements. I am also glad to hear that the news of the new client has stimulated you in your self-development, but you can still increase your cruising speed by several knots and keep working to sustain it. I suggest you look for the following document in Google: The Definitive 100 Most Useful Productivity Hacks, and that you try to incorporate some of the tips you learn so as to gain in productivity. You will need to improve it to move onto the next level of self-development.

Next week is critical. If you continue at a good pace, you will be ready to start with the next project, for the competency Digital Tools. I advance a suggestion for a specific objective. You could call it «digital cleaning». It would consist of spending a day simply ordering your digital tools. You may possibly need someone to help you.

Since I know that you like challenges, I pose you one on leadership: how about reframing your relationship with Helen by asking her to be your grand master for digital tools?

In preparation for this new project, I would suggest a book about how to learn to learn fast, a key competency to accelerate your self-development. Ultralearning: Accelerate Your Career, Master Hard Skills and Outsmart the Competition, by Scott H. Young.

Oliver

10th May | Boston | 21:44
Text message published on the platform

Good evening, Oliver,

What you ask me to do with Helen, more than a leadership challenge is a subtle and cruel form of torture. As expected, Andrea thinks it's an excellent idea. I will need your help to prepare that conversation. And I can't rule out that I may also need therapy to recover from it.

On the other hand, I confess that after the effort I have made in the last few weeks, I find it completely heartless of you to ask me to increase my cruising speed by several knots and to accelerate my self-development. I'll leave it there, for you to think about.

Sarah

11ᵗʰ May | Punta del Este | 15:32
Text message published on the platform

Good afternoon, Sarah,

Precisely because I greatly value the effort you are making in this programme and the achievements you are attaining in your self-development, I challenge you to give even more. The role of a mentor is not to win popularity contests or guarantee that mentees feel comfortable. Just the opposite: it consists of challenging them—in the most inspiring possible way—and provoking a healthy discomfort that inspires them to develop their own talent.

As you know, transformation hurts, like going on a diet or carrying out a demanding training programme. But at the present time, the risk of failing to accelerate in self-development and incorporating new competencies could be much more serious. And more painful. In the next few years, there is probably going to be an unprecedented wave of dismissals, particularly in large corporations. I will try to explain:

For more than a decade, a silent phenomenon has been taking place: the polarisation of talent. Due mainly to the acceleration effect of technology in transforming business models and systems of organisation, every day more sophisticated profiles are required in businesses and, at the same time, average profiles are more and more irrelevant. A large part of them will be replaced by automated processes or outsourced to countries with lower salary costs. It is true that today new jobs are also being created, but the growing tendency is towards highly specialised jobs (developers of applications or specialists in consultative sales, for example) or towards covering ever more necessary basic needs (local merchandise distributors or elderly people caregivers). Average professionals with average talent and a traditional academic background face the increasing risk of ending up being too expensive for the value they actually add to companies.

The basic assumption that in order to have access to the standard of living and to the benefits that the middle class has progressively attained, it is enough to obtain a degree at university, obtain a master's degree, enter the labour market and progress through an organisation at the pace of the training programmes provided by human resources departments, is being questioned by well-grounded studies that confirm the polarisation of talent. The question «which degree did you get and where» is becoming increasingly irrelevant. Today, the question is «what are you studying now, and how». In short, in the next decade, the capacity for self-development and for fast learning will largely determine professional career paths.

On the other hand, I know that you are enthusiastic about winning a new client and you have good reason to be so. But I would suggest caution when measuring the success of your consultative sales project: to measure it only in terms of the impact on the profit and loss account, due to the arrival of a new client, could well cloud the importance of working methodically to ensure the development of consultative sales competencies in each member of your team. It is the only way to ensure that capacity is installed in the organisation. And you know from your own experience that acquiring new competencies requires a large amount of learning and of discipline. Or, to put it briefly, it requires *#HeadHeartandHands*

I would suggest that during our next videoconference we should talk about how to cultivate your role as mentor of your team.

I wish you a good week with many *#achievements*

Oliver

Hi, Oliver. I have some good news and one piece of news which is terrible. I'm sending you this message from Miami Airport. I had been thinking about reporting my progress to you in writing, but something happened... Better if I first tell you my achievements of this week. It has been the first week in which I have met practically all the commitments that I made in my project for the competency Closeness and my two indicators have improved. What's more, I have continued with my progress in Habitify, both as regards my hours of sleep and my hours of reading. Ah, and also in sports: I have been out running three times this week. About the book *Ultralearning*, it is giving me very cool tips about how to learn fast. I still haven't finished it, but I have recommended it to all my team. Moreover, I do see the logic of reframing my relationship with Helen by asking her to help me to implement my project for Digital Tools and I have written to her to suggest that we talk. We have arranged to see each other next Wednesday. I will of course need some tips from you to prepare that conversation, which is not exactly going to be my favourite pastime. Until today, I would have said that I found that conversation difficult, but now, if I compare it with the conversation I have to have with Bryan, it's a piece of cake. *Oof...* How to explain this to you... Yesterday, Friday, I went down to Miami to spend the weekend with Bryan. He came on Wednesday for a medical congress, so we decided to stay over on the Saturday and Sunday, and we booked a room at the Mandarin Oriental. It was good for both of us. To rest together and reconnect, because in the last few months, with so much travel, our relationship has been... how can I say it... deteriorating. Last night we went for dinner at restaurant La Mar, run by Gastón Acurio, which is a place I love, and we thoroughly enjoyed ourselves. Early this morning I went running in Brickell, then we had breakfast together on the terrace of the hotel and afterwards we went to sunbathe at the pool. 'Till then, everything fine. But while I was lying on my beach bed listening to *Ultralearning* with my earphones, Bryan went for a swim. His phone suddenly rang, and I saw that a certain Jenny was calling. At first, I didn't give it any importance, but after a while the idea started running through my head: «Who is this Jenny who calls my husband on a Saturday? And why isn't her surname registered in Bryan's cell phone?». Anyhow, I was holding the phone in my hand when a few minutes later came a message from Jenny that said: «My shift today is really going to be a drag...». Well, I leaped off the beach bed, marched to the pool and, without waiting for him to leave the water, with his phone in my hand and with that vein in my forehead almost certainly protruding, I shouted at him: «Who's Jenny, eh? Eh? A girlfriend from the hospital?». And then Bryan asked me: «What are you talking about?». He tried to say something else, in fact, that I didn't even hear, because I picked up my things like lightning, went up to the room, made my suitcase, ordered an Uber and now I'm in the airport waiting to board the next flight back to Boston. *Oof...* I've already told Andrea, who did her best to calm me down, but I wanted to let you know too, before getting on the plane, how things went this week, including the way the party ended... I have about fifteen missed calls from Bryan, but I'm not in the mood to talk to him. Anyway, if you ever thought that this mentoring was going to be easy, there I go and leave you this mess... I don't know where to start to clean it up. Ciao.

18th May | Punta del Este | 08:06
Text message published on the platform

Good morning, Sarah,

Although very pleased with your *#achievements* of this week,

87

the episode with Bryan saddens me.

Your hurried flight from Miami, without giving him any opportunity to explain, demonstrates that your «juniority» keeps coming to the surface, but in a more important field, your private life. I would like to make several suggestions in this respect, based on my own errors and learning, but for the moment, I invite you to watch the talk *El poder de una conversación* on TED (this one was given in Spanish). It is also suitable for the conversation you have planned with Helen.

I, too, have some news. I am now officially a grandfather. Oliver has been born, the son of my daughter Alison, who lives in Madrid. Next week I will in fact be going to see them and I will connect to our videoconference from there. It is already planned for 28th May.

Oliver

22nd May | Copenhagen | 20:06
Text message published on the platform

Good evening, Oliver,

Congratulations on your grandson! I do think it's so considerate of them to give him your name... Please, do send me a photo. Returning to our mentoring, there is a lot to talk about, but I prefer to leave the sensitive subjects for our videoconference on 28th May. I would further propose that we postpone it until the 30th and that we actually see each other in Madrid. Quite by chance, I had planned a weekend break to see a friend in Madrid from the time when I was doing my MBA at IE. What do you think? Paloma has recently been appointed general manager of the InterContinental Hotel and she tells me they do a spectacular breakfast.

In my conversation with Helen, the TED about *El poder de una conversación* was very useful. Particularly, the model for preparing difficult conversations based on the capacity to put forward arguments and to generate empathy. I confess that things went more easily than I had imagined. It's not that we have become bosom friends, but now I think we can collaborate without sparks flying around at every interaction. I invited her to coffee, and we ended up talking for almost two hours. We concluded that she is a convergent thinker and that I tend to be a divergent thinker. And perhaps this explains to a large extent why we collide. And we also discovered that we have common interests: the last thing that I would have imagined is that Helen also likes dancing! Anyhow, this experience has been a learning process...

With whom I have not had a conversation is with Bryan. I told him that I wasn't ready to talk and that I needed time to think. At home we have lived like strangers since I returned from Copenhagen yesterday. I preferred to put the ocean between us, reorganising my travel agenda; next week I go to Berlin and to Madrid, and the week after to London. When I return to Boston, on 4th June, we'll see what happens.

As to my *#achievements* this week, the most important by far has been my conversation with Helen. And I have also implemented almost all my commitments for the competency Closeness. What surprises me is that closeness has taken me to provide feedback almost naturally and now I am actually not sure which one I am working on exactly. In any case, I think that I am ready to start to work on the competency of Digital Tools. I attach the project to review it with you before sending it to my «new friend» Helen. I have already sent it to Andrea and her feedback has been very useful to me.

SARAH | DIGITAL TOOLS

SELF DIAGNOSIS 1

Scale: 4 Excellent – 3 Good – 2 Fair – 1 Bad

PROBLEM/OPPORTUNITY

I use email and WhatsApp as my main tools for communication. I hardly know the Office 365 applications. I reply impulsively to all the different notifications that I receive. I am permanently overwhelmed by the amount of information I receive.

GENERAL OBJECTIVE

Develop a work system that allows me to coordinate the work of my team with agility and also to dedicate more time to one to two responsibilities on my agenda that I have overlooked due to my disordered attention to day to day activities: strategy and people development.

SPECIFIC OBJECTIVES

- Digital clean-up. Date: next week.
- **Workshop: New rules for digital collaboration.** Date: Before the end of the month.

TIME FRAME 60 days

IMPLEMENTATION

LEARNING RESOURCES

- *Leading Virtual Teams.* HBR Press
- *Virtual Collaboration.* HBR Press
- *Scaling a Transformative Culture Through a Digital Factory.* Digital Mckinsey
- *How Social Tools Can Reshape the Organization.* Digital Mckinsey

IMMEDIATE DECISIONS

- **Digital clean up.** Spend one day exclusively to cleaning my inbox, to organising it in files, to establishing rules for handling the emails I receive, to ordering all my documents, to synchronising my computer with my cellular phone, to adjusting the notifications I receive, to installing the company's collaborative tools, and to renewing my passwords.
- **Workshop:** New rules for digital collaboration. Spend half a day defining with my team which collaborative tools to use for different communication needs, identifying clear criteria and a disciplined follow up model.

DAILY AND WEEKLY PRACTISES

- No multitasking during meetings.
- Plan a specific time during the day for reviewing collaborative platforms.
- Plan a specific time in the week for digital clean up and organising information.

One more thing before closing: on Tuesday I had a meeting with the Vice President for Talent. We talked about my career path in the organisation and he mentioned that they are evaluating my appointment as Vice President for Sales, because my boss is in the process of taking early retirement. In general, I think that the interview went well. I told him about how our mentoring programme is going. He was very interested to know more about the particulars of the methodology. Although I think that there was something he didn't like: that I should share your model of Transformation Competencies with my team. He said that they were having difficulty implementing the organisation's official model of competencies and that he didn't want people to get mixed up. To be honest, when they were presented, they sounded good to me, but a bit stratospheric. The problem is that I don't even remember them, in spite of the fact that they are now also painted on the walls of the office, maybe because the mission, the vision and the corporate values are also painted. For me it's too much. You know well that large companies like large solutions and end up introducing excessive complexity.

I look forward to hearing from you that you can make it for breakfast at the InterContinental Hotel on 30th May. I would love us to meet without the mediation of technology. As you know, I prefer personal interactions. Face to face.

Sarah

22nd May | Punta del Este | 18:35
Text message published on the platform

It sounds very good to me, Sarah. We will see each other on 30th May at 09:00. Your conversation with Helen is a sensational achievement. I also advance that your project for Digital Tools is very well planned.

Oliver

Conversation at the InterContinental Hotel

—Sarah?

—Oliver! What a pleasure to see you in person!

—Well, the same to you! How was your trip? Shall we sit down here?

—Yes, alright. I have been ten days between Copenhagen and Berlin. I really wanted to come to Madrid. I'm staying at my friend Paloma's home. She lives close by, in Chamberi. And you?

—At my daughter Alison's house, in Velazquez Avenue.

—By the way, congratulations for little Oliver! How is he?

—Thank you very much. He's fine. He was an early delivery, so he was small at birth, but he has recovered his weight. Here I have a photo.

—Oh, he's gorgeous! How cute! And your daughter, she's so pretty!

—So is her mother. Well, we have several things to talk about today.

—Well, yes. And quite honestly, I don't know where to begin.

—Let me help you. What have you learned about the conversation with Helen?

—That I made a rash judgement of her. At heart, what I didn't like about her were not her defects but her virtues.

—Why?

—Because I'm very competitive and my tendency is to show my claws to anyone who is a threat.

—And Helen is a threat?

—Maybe not, but we joined the company at the same time and it annoys me that she is on the executive committee—although she isn't vice president—and she has greater access than me to Claus in spite of the fact that, in the last few years, I have achieved results that he has categorised several times as outstanding; whilst Helen only works in supporting areas, like finance and risk. Said like that, directly and without filters... I was—and maybe I still am—a bit jealous of her.

—I congratulate you. That reflection reveals a higher degree of maturity than when you started the programme. What do you think that is due to?

—More exactly, to whom: to Covey, to Aristotle... Even to Agassi. In the time I have been doing the programme, I have read more than in the last five years. That intellectual diet has made me think and, what's more, it has been food for my conversations with Andrea.

—I would like to meet her one day. She seems to be very sensible. And a very good friend.

—You would be delighted to know her. Andre is the best!

—And with Bryan, don't you talk about these things?

—...

—Does that mean no?

—At the beginning, yes. But for some time... I don't know, he is so involved in his hospital, in his life... It's as though we don't have much in common anymore.

—I see. I don't know of any married couple that at some time hasn't gone through something like that.

—Including your marriage?

—Including mine.

—And how do you get over it? With therapy?

—I suppose it would depend on each case. Sometimes, it's enough for a good friend to listen to you and to tell you some things that you don't want to hear.

—Such as?

—Perhaps you have brought home a large number of the bricks with which you and your partner are building that wall that separates you. Or at least, to a greater extent than you thought.

—Define brick.

—Excessive dedication to work, little conversation, digital isolation, you see your series and I see mine...

—With those three you can put a tick against my name.

93

—It's within your own reach to remove that tick and to go back to having conversations, to making special plans, to redesigning together your family project...

—Something like an «offsite meeting» for strategic planning with your partner?

—Could be. But like any good offsite meeting, it needs to be well prepared beforehand.

—How?

—Not with anything spectacular. With small affectionate gestures. Every day.

—Even though I don't feel like it at all.

—That enhances the value of it. That's real love.

—...

—What's the matter, Sarah?

—I have more than thirty missed calls from Bryan.

—Perhaps you overdid it at the Mandarin Oriental.

—Do you think so?

—As one of my friends says: «That problem needs a conversation». Give him the opportunity to explain. It might be something serious or it might be that your imagination has exaggerated the facts.

—I'll think about it.

—Sarah, why don't you design a project for Closeness with Bryan? In the past few months, you have accomplished some formidable achievements with your team.

—Oh yes, of course. You solve everything with projects. And you see eeeverything as easy.

—I know from experience that it isn't.

—O.K. Then I need you to talk to me about your own experience.

—It might disconcert you.

—I don't care.

—Alright, Sarah. What I'm going to tell you is not particularly edifying. And there's no turning back. Are you quite sure?

—Absolutely.

—Many years ago, I was offered the opportunity to move to Miami and from there to carry out the expansion in Latin America of the company for which I was then working. At that time, we lived in London and Valentina thought it was an opportunity, amongst other things, to be nearer her parents and to go and visit them more frequently in Uruguay. So we started organising our new life in Miami: we rented a house in Key Biscayne, we found a school, we contacted with some friends who lived there... From the outside, everything seemed perfect. But during those years, as a result of a dramatic family incident, I was broken inside. My heart was not with Valentina. It was centred on my work and, at the same time, dispersed in minor— and sometimes serious—adventures with women from work or from elsewhere.

—This is beginning to get exciting...

—The day arrived when I had to move to Miami. The family would come several months later, as planned. The day I left, just before boarding the flight to Miami at Heathrow, I sent an email to my latest «adventure», telling her that what we had lived together in the last few weeks was the most extraordinary thing that had ever happened to me and assuring her that I would find a way to embark on a new life together. Hours later, she replied to me deeply moved, but the way I received her reply was frankly humiliating. I had left my iPad at home in London and Valentina had been looking for something when a notification of a new message appeared in my Hotmail.

—Oh my God...

—When I was waiting for my luggage at the airport, Valentina called me, read me the emails and said to me, with astounding self-composure, that she felt very deeply disillusioned. In the following months, I went into a free fall.

—I bet you did.

—One day I was having dinner with a good friend at The Rusty Pelican restaurant, in Key Biscayne, with views across the bay to downtown Miami. It was a very crude conversation. He told

95

me exactly what he thought: that I had become an addict for fast-food emotions, that my will power was weakened in extreme, that I lived in such an entirely self-centred manner that I wasn't capable of perceiving the damage I was doing to Valentina and to my daughters.

—That friend of yours sounds just like Andrea.

—Perhaps so. And he defied me to ask Valentina for her forgiveness and to give my life to win her heart again. To me, it sounded like such a Herculean task that was completely beyond my power. At that point in my life, I had broken more things than I would have time to mend... Then he asked me: «Are you capable right now of jumping into the water and swimming across the bay to downtown?» My reply was categorically negative. «And would you be capable—he insisted—of swimming to that wooden post, that must be about three hundred yards away?» «That far, yes», I replied.

—Very shrewd, your friend.

—«Start by breaking off that relation immediately and radically—he said to me—and when you get that far, go and ask Valentina to forgive you. And later on, you will discover the next thing you have to do».

—And did she forgive you?

—It took her some time. But when she did, she did so completely. She gave me a backpack and she said: «Let's begin a new journey. With the backpack empty but with more experience».

—Forgive me, Oliver, but I don't understand. How can anyone forgive something like that? And so promptly?

—To the first question, the most precise answer is that Valentina is an extraordinary woman. About the second question, I would say that forgiveness is a process. And forgiving someone else is often surprisingly easier than to forgive yourself. It took me quite a time. In those years, I did a master's degree in human misery...

—And how did you manage it?

—Valentina's unconditional forgiveness broke me up... One day she recommended a book to me, Wounds in the Heart, the Healing Power of Forgiveness, by Dr. Schlatter. And that day I realised that she was ready. It was only me that still had to get up out of the mud.

—To be ready. I wish it were as easy as it sounds...

—So do I.

—...

—Sarah, you have got something there.

—Here, on my blouse? Where? I can't see it.

—No. There inside. In your heart.

—What do you mean?

—What's the matter with your mother?

—...

—What's the matter, Sarah?

—I had promised myself I would never open that strongbox... in all my life. I had buried it at the bottom of the sea, far from the coast, as though it were highly dangerous radioactive material. And now... it's as though the tides had brought it back to the coast and the ocean had dashed it against the rocks to break it open. And then just a few waves were enough to leave it on the shore, broken and exposed... My mother...

—Use my handkerchief.

—...

—Take your time.

I'm OK now. Thank you.

—What's the matter with your mother, Sarah?

—I suppose it's my turn now. I had the fortune to grow up on one of the most beautiful country estates in Llanogrande, a lovely place where many families from Medellin come up to spend the weekend. I lived there with my parents, my brother and my grandmother, who was the owner and the heart and soul of the place. And there we also spent Christmas and holidays. I loved to go out riding early with my grandmother and to go and see the flowers cultivated there. My grandmother taught me the names of all of them. And she gave them nicknames: «It looks as if the conceited orchids haven't woken up today», or «how beautiful those tousled dahlias are...». My grandmother was so unique... She never stopped working all her life and she earned that estate with the sweat of her brow. My mother inherited everything except the genetics for work. She spent money as if there were no tomorrow and she lived life immoderately, with all possible luxuries and satisfying all her whims. My grandmother suffered a great deal with my mother and, when she went, we realised that only she had been able to restrain her. When my mother drank too much, my grandmother sent her to the guest house and forbade us to go near her with a terse and severe: «your mother is indisposed». That meant that we wouldn't see her until the following day, which she usually spent in bed. Sometimes, she was so bad that we had to send for the doctor. My grandmother died when I was twelve years old. For my fifteenth birthday, my mother organised a party that was talked about in the whole of Antioquia. She even brought a singer who was in fashion from Madrid. Two hundred guests attended, and I felt like the Queen of Sheba. The party continued according to plan and frankly, I lost sight of my mother for a couple of hours. The problem was when she reappeared in the midst of the party, completely drunk and half naked, in front of the guests and—even worse— in front of my friends. At first, I felt unbearably humiliated and, then, a mixture of pity and contempt.

—I can well imagine.

—Since then, my relationship with her progressively deteriorated and the day I was eighteen years old I moved away as far as possible and went to study my university degree at the Tec of Monterrey. At first, I only went back for Christmas, that festive season that lifts people's spirits or sinks them in misery, depending on how they get on with their family. But since I married Bryan, I don't even go.

—And how are your father and your brother?

—My father always sought refuge in work and now he seeks refuge in golf. I don't blame him. My mother's health deteriorated with each passing day and now she lives in their house in Medellin, attended day and night by two carers. When she sometimes skips her medication or drinks beyond the limits the doctor imposes on her, she has to be hospitalised for a few days. My brother lives in Bogota with his family and goes to see her some weekends.

—And you?

—The last time was six years ago.

—...

—I know what you're going to say. But... no thank you.

—Why?

—In the first place, because I don't feel like it at all. And secondly because, in the event of seeing her, I wouldn't have time to say loud and clear all the things I want to say to her.

—And if you only had sixty seconds to talk to her, what would you say?

—...

—Perhaps you could begin by thanking her for all the good things she has given you. That includes your own life.

—I can see that you are about to ask me to take a backpack and give it to her as a present.

—Rather than that, perhaps you might be understanding with the decline produced by an addiction like alcoholism and with the hell lived out by those who fall into it.

—There's no doubt about that. Anything else? I would still have about twenty seconds

—All yours.

—...

—Sarah, what would you say to your mother in those last twenty seconds?

—Maybe something about how I have treated her. What was the title of that book that Valentina recommended you?

—Wounds in the Heart.

—I have a few of those.

—Sarah, we are running out of time and we haven't talked about you Digital Tools project, but I only have one comment.

—What?

—It is very well designed: Implement it with a little more discipline than you have used in the last few weeks.

—You are incorrigible!

—That's not true. Thank God, I was. Otherwise, Valentina would have left me.

—Good point. And what do you recommend me to do to take up my role as mentor of my team?

—Mindsight, by Daniel Siegel. It's a book that will help you to know yourself and to know them in more depth. It introduces very practical tools for transforming behaviour anchored in the passage of many years or to get rid of that irrational fear that sometimes tortures us and blocks us.

—Another book that sounds as if it was written for me.

—I hope you enjoy it.

—And you your grandson. I don't want to rob you of any more of your time.

—Thank you.

—Ciao.

4th June | Boston | 23:03
Text message published on the platform

Good evening, Oliver,

Just back in Boston, I have three new things to tell you. The first is that this afternoon I tried to have a conversation with Bryan, and it didn't turn out as I had expected... He assured me that he and Jenny are friends, nothing else. The second is that I have just bought an air ticket to Medellin. And the third is that what you discovered in my heart about my mother has now gone down to my stomach. In the form of a knot.

Sarah.

(Four months later)

Text message published on the platform

Good evening, Oliver,

Today, it is eight months since I started the programme. The time has simply flown by so quickly! It seems incredible that in a month's time we will have finished... Here are my *#achievements* for this week:

- About the Diagnosis and Decision competency, I have now finished the book, Thinking, Fast and Slow, by Daniel Kanheman. Clearly, I have the challenge to domesticate the system #1 in my brain (automatic and impulsive) by strengthening the muscle of my system #2 (conscious and focussed). For that purpose, I'm doing the reframing exercise explained by Dr. Majeres in his video Optimal Work. I found it on YouTube.
- My team is enthusiastic about the self-development workshop we held in Berlin on Monday and about the dynamics we have set up with the Workplace tool to share learning experiences and resources. As you suggested, we have all agreed to publish weekly some #achievement in the competencies that each is working on. It's so cool that this dynamic of self-development is collaborative, that we can share with the team our development challenges, the #achievements that each one is attaining, the resources (books, documents, videos, podcasts, apps, etc.) that are useful for each person... I really think that this model for managing talent should be exported to the rest of the organisation, maybe when we have more experience implementing it. For the moment, my team has started with a lot of #head and #heart. But I am watchful to see what happens next week, to alert those who have difficulty in getting things down to their #hands. They already know that

«transformation hurts». But anyway, although my team is enthusiastic, I am trying to conceal my insecurity, because it's the first time that I have taken the plunge to facilitate a workshop on a subject outside my area of expertise.

- I don't know whether it counts for our programme, but Bryan has taken me on as his mentor for digital tools and I spend Saturday afternoon teaching him to install and use the new collaborative platforms that have been introduced at his hospital. By the way, he continues to make his best efforts to win my heart again. He sends me messages all day, he calls me at the office, he even leaves me notes in the fridge...

Next week I will be meeting the Vice President for Talent in Boston. This is the key meeting. I'll tell you how it goes.

Sarah

17th October | Punta del Este | 12:32
Text message published on the platform

Good morning, Sarah,

Today, Saturday, we have some lovely spring weather in Punta and Valentina and I took advantage of it this morning to take a walk with the dogs along Playa Brava.

I didn't want to wait until Monday to tell you that you can't imagine just how pleased I am about your *#achievements* this week. Most particularly, that you have decided to implement our methodology of self-development with your team. You have made progress at a good pace during these months and you are now ready to replicate it. Good luck in your meeting with the Talent VP.

Oliver

Damn it, Oliver! I'm completely shattered! In the last eight months I have worked on my self-development more than I have ever done in all my life. I've disciplined myself with Habitify, I'm sleeping more than seven hours a day, I run three times a week, I don't eat between meals, stuffing myself with chocolate has come to an end. I unsubscribed from Netflix and I downloaded Audible, I have read twenty books, including that of your friend Aristotle, which is not exactly the reading you find at the hairdresser, and even Crime and Punishment by Dostoevsky. I have lost count of how many TED talks and YouTube videos I have watched, I have developed my project on Closeness, another one for Digital Tools and yet another for Diagnosis and Decision, and I have given more feedback than in all my professional life. But that's not an exhaustive list, no, no, many more things have happened, some of them of a transcendental nature: I have saved my relation with Bryan— if it weren't for all the conversations we have had, it is more than likely that we would be living apart like perfect strangers—although, to be fair, he is also doing what he can and with me he displays the patience of Job. It's still a long way from being a flowing relationship, but we keep going... Then there's the question of my mother. You can't imagine the size of the knot I had inside. And I still think it's a miracle that we were able to reconcile and that I was able to accompany her in her last hours... Oh, the poor thing! It was such a pity to see her go in such a deplorable state, nothing but skin and bone, and with that so very faint voice, but which said such beautiful things to me before it faded away. Oh God!

(...)

Excuse me for my emotion... These have been such intense months, a long distance race, with my eyes always on the target, without any concessions to myself, increasing the pace each week, until it became a constant go, go, go, that started in my head, then went down to my heart and now comes out from my hands so naturally, as a habit, as if it requires no effort, but I know—and I know that you know—that I have put my life into this programme... So all I needed was for the Talent VP to come and tell me, with insufferable paternalism, that they greatly value my efforts, that they are very pleased with my results and with my volume of sales, but that they don't see me yet as Vice President for Sales, that they have decided to bring in someone from outside; and on the part of Claus, thank you for everything, and I shouldn't be worried, they still see me with future projection... as a high-potential.

(...)

Oliver, we have failed. Both of us. All this effort to gain seniority and to be vice president has been useless. And you know what? I'm fed up. I've had enough. This lesson has been too expensive. But I have learned it in my own flesh, and it has been engraved on me with fire. That's how the corporate world is. Ungrateful and cold. As cold as a fish. So, with the same coldness, tomorrow morning I will hand in my letter of resignation to Claus. I'm going to draw it up tonight. Damn it!

Text message published on the platform

Good evening, Oliver,

Before writing my letter of resignation, I wanted to ask you to forgive me for the message I sent you this morning. I was blind with rage, just having left the office of the Vice President for Talent. I know it's not your fault. You don't deserve to be spoken to like that, after all that you have done to help me during these past months... I just want you to know that I am deeply disappointed with my organisation. I feel as though my car had left the road at top speed due to a badly signed curve and turned over seventeen times...

Sarah

23rd October | Punta del Este | 06:09
Audio message published on the platform

Good morning, Sarah. I didn't sleep well last night. I was uneasy, without knowing why. I woke up with the first ray of sunlight and I have just seen your messages. Instead of writing to you, this time I preferred to come down to the beach with the dogs, and from here, sitting on the sand, contemplating a serenely epic daybreak, I want to tell you about something that has been living inside me for the last fourteen years. I don't only have two children. I have three. The eldest, Oliver, would now be twenty-eight. He was the first to appear. Our boy. He was a man of few words. With a discreet sensitivity. He was sparing in his exterior manifestations of affection, but he had a passionate heart. He was adventurous, but he didn't share his sense of adventure with everyone. His group of friends was small, and he brought them home frequently. They were devoted to him. They produced several inventions down in the basement. Oliver liked maps and they planned exotic trips together, indicating the route with coloured drawing pins to identify shelters for provisions. He also read a great deal, especially adventure books. Every night before going to bed, I had to take a book carefully from his hands and turn out the light. He did well at school. He obtained grades that even the most demanding father would be proud of. He was calm, until someone suddenly hit the wrong key and woke the monster. One day he took on three boys older than himself because they had laughed at his sister Claire. He came home with a bleeding nose but without any complaint, proud of having defended my daughter from three bullies. Alison and Claire had a mixture of admiration and fear for their elder brother, because he had a surprising ability to persuade them to try out his inventions. You can imagine how the hanging doll's house ended up, and I still don't know how he convinced them to go inside. Valentina had a very special relationship with him, very intimate. He admired me. He thought I must be very important because I travelled a lot. He implored me to take him with me on my business trips and I promised him that, when he was fourteen, he would come with me. At that time, I was working on a project in Switzerland, so we planned a weekend excursion to the Alps. We rented a room in a small house near the village of Grindelwald, located opposite the Eiger, an impressive mountain of over thirteen thousand feet. It was early March. The valley was completely covered with snow. Oliver was excited because it was the first time he had travelled alone with his father, and moreover, to the mountains. We arrived at the house on Friday and the owners received us with the fire burning and a fabulous dinner. On Saturday, we did some cross-country skiing and on Sunday, we got up early to go up to the foot of the mountain. High enough to be able to contemplate the valley from above and say farewell to it before our return journey. We first went to the house to pick up our luggage and say goodbye to the family and around four o'clock we left. We had rented a 4 x 4 at Zurich airport, well equipped for mountain roads, and the snowploughs had done an excellent job. Since we were in good time, we decided to drive on secondary roads to enjoy the views. We must have been driving something more than half an hour when I asked Oliver to put on a CD with the music we had recorded for the trip. He said that it was on the back seat, in his backpack, and I asked him to reach back for it. From the back seat, he passed me the CD and said to me: «I recorded this with your music for the return trip». Whilst I put it on, I was distracted for a second and when I raised my eyes, I was on the wrong side of the road with an approaching lorry only yards away. I turned the steering sharply and we veered off the road. The car turned over several times and when it came to a stop, Oliver wasn't in the car. I scrambled out the best I could shouting «Oliver! Where are you? Are you alright? Oliver!». But the cold echo of the valley only returned my own words to me. I tried to climb back up to the road, rock by rock, until I saw blood, very slowly soaking the snow, and then I saw my son, lying as though he were asleep... The engine had stopped, but from the car, with disconcerting irony, came the sound of *The Long and Winding Road*.

(...)

Sarah, I am sure that you will now believe me if I say that I know how you feel about the news they have given you. In Boston you are an hour behind, and you will probably hear my message on the subway, on your way to the office. Pay attention to what I am going to say now: tear up that damned letter, throw it into the first litter bin you find, when you enter the office say good morning to whomsoever you may see, go to your office, open your computer, look at what you have on your agenda and spend the day serving your team, your colleagues and your clients. With all humility, but as though you were the owner of the company. Then take a rest at the weekend with

Bryan and, next week, tell me how your team is getting on with their self-development. From now on, their achievements will also be yours.

Text message published on the platform

Good morning, Oliver,

I did it. When I came out of the subway at Park Street, I didn't only tear up the letter, I think that I was also torn up inside and now I am looking for the pieces...

On Monday, changes were announced in the organisation. They have created a new vice presidency for Helen. I went to see her to congratulate her. Everyone now knows that my accelerated career in the company has veered off on one of the curves of this *long and winding road*.

Oliver, I really am terribly sorry for making you re-live the accident... I am not a person of faith. Or if I have any faith, it's locked up in one of the chests at my grandmother's estate. But for the past few days, I have the certainty that is more solid than this table: your son Oliver is helping me from up there, wherever he may be. I talk to him and he listens to me. I can feel it. In a way I can't describe.

Today I came to the office early. I have a round of calls with my team, to check their self-development plans. I am going to need all the energy I can muster.

Sarah

28th October | Punta el Este | 22:51
Audio message published on the platform

Sarah, now it's me who's going to need some kind of help. All of this has suddenly broken me up again... I thought the pieces had been solidly stuck back together, like a contact glue that lets you put the pieces together, press them, count to three, and there they are, forever together again, as though they had never been separated... Sarah, neither am I a man of faith. I have always been an agnostic in respect of anything that is not my own capacity to solve problems. In fact, my agnosticism is proportional to Valentina's faith, which is solid as a rock. Valentina has the house full of photos of our son and she says that she talks to him, that she feels he is present in some way—how would I know—mystically. In the same way as she talks to Jesus and to the Virgin Mary, she also talks to Oliver. And I love her—I owe her my life!—and I respect her, but I don't understand anything. Nothing! Perhaps I have never wanted to understand it. But now you, suddenly, just like that, out of the sky and without any warning, you say that you are talking to my Oliver... with my little boy... my God... Sarah... I can't go on ... forgive me...

30th October | Boston | 19:11
Audio message published on the platform

Good afternoon, Oliver. I have just arrived home. Yesterday was a very intense day and I hadn't listened to your message until now. It touched me very deeply... With your pieces and with mine, scattered around the floor, it's as if a child has been playing distractedly with all his toys without putting any of them away. If I think about it, some of your pieces are useful to me if I join them to mine. Maybe friendship consists of exchanging pieces. Like kids who exchange football cards, or marbles. Oliver, I'm going ahead with your plan: forgetting about my failure and focusing on serving my team, my colleagues and my clients. But I am only groping forward in the dark, like when you get up in the night and you don't want to put the light on so as not to wake up, and you feel your way along the walls and get back into bed in the same position so that your sleep doesn't evaporate. And I have a recurring nightmare, in which all the executive committee appears, laughing heartily at me, without any restraint, almost falling out of their chairs, when I enter the meeting room by mistake and the Vice President for Talent tells me that I have come to the wrong meeting, that the meeting for high-potentials is on the floor below. Better not tell you what I say to him, which is when I wake up agitated and Bryan asks me if I'm alright, and I tell him to shut up, poor man, as if he were to blame... But I keep going, managing the business and accompanying my team in their self-development process. This week they have sent me their first projects and I am in the process of giving them feedback. Although there are two who haven't sent me anything and I'm thinking about sending them an explosive message like yours, telling them that if they aren't prepared to work with discipline, they can leave the programme. I look at myself a year ago and I wonder if I am overcoming my juniority. Oliver, I'm beginning to miss you and we still haven't finished our mentoring, although I know what you're going to say in your next message: our last videoconference is programmed for 11th November. There's almost nothing left... Oh God!

3rd November | Punta del Este | 08:12
Text message published on the platform

Good morning, Sarah,

First of all, my apologies for my last message. It was inappropriate. I shouldn't have sent it to you. It transgresses our methodology.

114

I indeed confirm that our last videoconference is programmed for 11th November. And at that time, by design, we will follow a debriefing plan, a format that helps to focus on the essential things you have learned and to anchor them. So that you can start preparing, I advance this question: what do you to take away from this programme?

On the other hand, I would recommend that you don't send those explosive messages to your colleagues. You have developed a sufficient degree of closeness with them to call them and ask them why they haven't met their commitment to publish their projects in Workplace. Listen to them carefully. If anyone's reply is related to the human fragility of understanding (head), wanting (heart), but not finding the time to do (hands), offer help by suggesting a new delivery date. As early as possible. But perhaps you will find that someone prefers to go it alone, without the commitment to publish *#achievements*. Frequently, they will be people particularly orientated to operations, with a technical profile and with little interest in teams. A habitual symptom is that they don't hold conversations about strategy with their peers. They prefer to «cook» everything with their boss. It is a good idea to help these people to understand that they are limiting themselves to being just managers, and that the self-development programme you are implementing, with its dynamic of collaborative learning, presents them with a magnificent opportunity to contribute to the team not only with their technical knowledge. If, after a couple more spaced out conversations, they continue to prefer to go it alone, that is the moment to invite them to leave the programme and, in some cases, which you will have to evaluate prudently, to leave the team as well.

This is the last week of the programme and it is the time for putting the final touches. I look forward to seeing you publish your *#achievements* on Friday.

One more thing. I think it's the appropriate time to read *Unbroken*, by Laura Hillenbrand. It will be useful for you to confront the coming months.

Oliver

6th November | London | 21:12
Text message published on the platform

Good evening, Oliver.

Since this is the last written message that I will publish on the platform, allow me the license to say that in the same manner as sticking to the methodology during these nine months has, in my case, transformed me as a leader and as a person, in your case, I think it would do you good to skip it occasionally. It may surprise you to hear that your moments of divergence have been a frankly inspiring counterpoint for me.

I summarise the most significant *#achievements* for this week:

- I am reading Mark Divine's book, that you recommended several months ago, Unbeatable Mind. The importance that the Navy Seals give to controlling the way you breathe is a genuine discovery for me. Quick conclusion: although it is almost humiliating to know that at this time of life I still didn't know how to breathe, the technique I have learned is helping me to keep my brain more lucid and with a more serene state of mind. As a specific objective, I have resolved to apply the technique before each meeting and before each conversation. For the moment, my success rate is twenty per cent. By the way, I have put Unbroken on my wish list.

- I have also reviewed the competency projects for each person in my team. Except one, Frank, who has already asked me a couple of times to excuse him. He says he has a lot of work and that, although he thinks self-development is an important subject, he prefers to do it by himself without publishing #achievements in our group on Workplace. Following your recommendation, I talked to him yesterday and gave him my arguments for working on his self-development collaboratively with the rest of the team. I asked him to think about it and that in a month's time we'll see how far he has advanced alone.

I am preparing my reflections for the final debriefing. I will connect from Copenhagen.

Sarah

11th November | Copenhagen – 19:00 | Punta del Este – 14:00
Videoconference

—Hi Oliver, how are you?
—Very well, Sarah. I see that you are on tour again.
—That's right. Tomorrow I travel to Berlin to be close to my team. And to our clients.
Maybe I should move around the corporate offices more but, as you will understand, that's not my priority at present.
—I understand. And although it may sound counterintuitive, if you maintain those priorities it is possible that your results— and I'm not referring to sales figures—will end up opening the way to higher responsibilities for you in your organisation. Or perhaps in another.
—Who knows. Here, I'm afraid there isn't much more opportunity for me to grow.

—If there is anything that you have done in these months, Sarah, it is to grow.

—Certainly not in the last few weeks.

—In the last few weeks, you have probably grown more than in the whole programme. But inside.

—I don't understand. What do you mean?

—What's happening to you is like those high mountain trees. When winter comes and the snow piles up on their branches, they cannot feed themselves from photosynthesis and they look for food by extending their roots between the rocks. And precisely those strong roots allow them to stand firm under storms and lightning. But when spring arrives, and it always arrives, they are a spectacle of flowers and fruit.

—I only wish that someday I'll be able to invite you to that spring festival. At present, I only feel that this process of professional grief is taking on a life of its own that is stirring me up inside, my beliefs, my expectations... even my priorities.

—For example?

—Bryan was very low on the list but, little by little, he's moving up. I am beginning to think that he wasn't altogether unfaithful, that maybe he only behaved with too much familiarity with that Jenny. Maybe he reacted like any castaway heart, desperate enough to drink from the nearest water, the sea water, which is always harmful... And meanwhile I was far away, floundering on my own, too occupied with my project, with my relentless career... I think we are in transition.

—I am very pleased to hear that, Sarah. It looks as though it's going in the right direction. And what else are you going to take away from this programme. Let's move into the debriefing.

—O.K. I've prepared it. I've come with ten conclusions. Nothing will be new to you, almost certainly. The important thing for me is that these basics are now inside me. I have lived them.

—I'm all ears.

—One. I am the person mainly responsible for my own self-development. Human resources could be a partner in support. And my boss, a mentor who guides me and challenges me, if he has the right qualities.

—Good.

—Two. As leader, I am also responsible for the development of my team. And I can't delegate that responsibility to human resources. But nobody can give what they haven't got: to be a mentor of something, first of all you have to learn yourself.

—Very good.

—Three. Without a method, the pace of learning is very slow and, probably, intermittent. But it must be simple, a quality that is infrequent in large organisations, which tend towards over-engineering and to creating an unnecessary degree of complexity.

—Interesting.

—Four. People are not transformed by listening to motivational talks or through academic tourism, but through learning by doing. That's why a project mentality is essential for self-development, carrying out small pilot schemes, experimenting, having a set of simple indicators to measure your success.

—Nothing to add.

—Five. Transformation hurts. If the muscle fibre isn't damaged, muscles don't grow. If the mentor doesn't create a healthy, permanent discomfort, he isn't doing his job properly.

—I'm happy to have created it.

—Six. The most important task of a leader is to build his own character, which is like the engine room for inspiration. And character depends on habits and habits depend on actions and actions depend on beliefs. Beliefs are installed in the mind in a complex manner, due to many stimuli. But in adult life, a determinant stimulus is the intellectual diet.

—Wow!

—Seven. The quality of your intellectual diet determines the quality of your leadership. Reading an adequate selection of books can change your perspectives of your professional life and, more importantly, of your personal life.

—Your case is a clear example.

—Eight. In order to inspire, it isn't necessary to live an impeccable life, but a life of endeavour. Every day, in small details. And this is much easier said than done.

—You're dead right.

—Nine. We put our lives on the line with the conversations that we hold. And sometimes with those that we don't hold. With the rhythm at which we live today, it's easy to neglect pending conversations and even easier to postpone them. But there is no greater transformation tool than a face to face conversation.

—Hear, hear!

—And ten. Traditional management competencies are not enough when extraordinary changes have to be tackled: like how to reinvent business models, or redesign complex processes, or restore deteriorated relations, or recapture the enthusiasm of a tired team. In summary, nowadays there is no lack of managers, but lack of leaders with the capacity to transform. And I thought I was a transformational leader until this mentoring programme put me in my place.

—And which is that place?

—I'm an apprentice.

—I wish to inform you that we are in the same place.

—So now it's my turn. What do you take away from this programme?

—I take away the pleasant surprise of having seen you grow at an unusual pace over these nine months—in spite of the fact that your application email wasn't very promising—and the conviction that you have interiorised that the goal of this programme was not a promotion to vice president but your personal transformation.

—So you can see that you shouldn't be deceived by appearances. What else?

—I take away a number of good practices of yours that will serve as examples for future mentoring processes.

—I'm glad to hear it.

—And I take away the satisfaction that you are implementing this methodology in your own team. I am sure that, with time, you will be an extraordinary mentor.

—I would like that, but I'm not sure if I'll ever be able to make this methodology really mine. How much of you is part of it?

—Everything, and at the same time, nothing. How do you distinguish between those beads of sweat on your forehead that slip down your nose and are eventually soaked up by your shirt, from the torrential rain that suddenly falls, like a gift, as unexpected as life itself?

— ...

—Sarah, it's time to finish.

—Wait. Now I know what my mentor takes away from this programme, but I ask myself what Oliver has gained from this journey.

—That question doesn't form part of the methodology.

—Right now, as far as I'm concerned, to hell with the methodology! What have you gained?

—...

—I have never seen you without words.

—I have the impression that my purpose has worn out.

—What!

—Like when a suit is too small, but you realise too late, when you have already left home. And you spend the day pulling down the sleeves, clasping them between the fingers and the palm of the hand. But it doesn't work. As soon as you put your cuffs on the table at that important business lunch, the shirt sleeves candidly appear, unmasking the fact that you need to visit your tailor.

—I don't see it like that. I think your purpose in life is very powerful: to contribute to the transformation of organisations through the transformation of people.

—But what has happened in the last few weeks leaves me pensive; not about the power of my purpose, but its depth. I suppose that it is possible to go deeper than I thought in personal transformation.

—Astonishing! The transformer needs a transformation.

—I think I am entering a transition phase as well.

—Oliver, I wouldn't want to miss it. Will we remain in contact?

—We will. What plans do you have for Christmas?

—I will go down to Medellin with Bryan, to spend Christmas with my father and brother. And you?

—I only know that Valentina is organising a family trip for our anniversary.

—I hope you relax. Grant yourself permission to celebrate life. Without any methodology.

—Sarah, our time has run out. Although the transformation continues. I wish you a good journey.

—Thank you, Oliver. Thank you for everything.

(Three months later)

Good morning, Oliver. I hope Valentina and yourself are very well. I have had you in my thoughts during these last few months... So many things have happened... There is so much to tell you. But I'll leave it until we plan a videoconference, like old times. I just want to advance some great news. We have started a new project, completely new and much more challenging than anything previous. But it isn't with my team, but with Bryan. We are expecting a baby.

PART TWO

Methodology for self-development

Over the last fifteen years, at **emergap** we have contributed to transforming more than a hundred companies in thirty countries, in Europe and America. The experience of helping them with our methodology to advance at a good pace in transforming their businesses and their organisations in depth—whilst continuing to manage day to day operations—has been a formidable source of learning from which, in the first place, we ourselves benefit, in addition to the companies we serve. That is to say, we find ourselves working in a permanent orbit of receiving, thanking, processing and delivering. But by far the most fascinating experience we have acquired during these years has been accompanying thousands of professional people in their personal transformation.

At the beginning, progressively surprised by the stories of human development that unfolded during these journeys of transformation, we adopted a focus that was both spontaneous and experimental, whereby we suggested things to read, videos to watch and certain best practices to implement which we had observed in extraordinary people with whom we have had the privilege to work. We then decided to create a **Self-development Programme** which we now implement both in the companies that engage our complete consulting model—design of transformation strategy, anchor it in a portfolio of projects, implement them under the leadership of middle managers and, on the other hand, develop competencies in the leaders of the organisation—and in the companies that already have their transformation in progress but feel that the development of their leaders is not progressing at an adequate pace. These two different speeds generate a large amount of frustration, like trying to walk on a treadmill belt that is moving at ten miles an hour.

Below, we introduce the ten basic principles of our model for self-development, which have appeared gradually in the course of the book and, later, a description of the key moments in the *mentoring* process.

10 principles for self-development

1. Each person is the protagonist of his or her own development. It is not a responsibility that can be delegated. Until a couple of decades ago, access to education and training was blocked by a barricade which companies largely overcame by allocating a budget to the human resources department. The barricade has been removed in recent years: the quantity and quality of educational and training resources available, for the most part free of charge or at a very low cost, have multiplied exponentially. Two inertias remain, however. The first of them is that in spite of the fact that these areas are now usually called Learning & Development, the focus of traditional training continues to be mainly on content. The second is that many executives and professionals continue to delegate their own development to the human resources department of the company where they work. The most practical way to make a clean break with both tendencies is to introduce a new capacity into the organisation: self-development. Starting with senior management.

2. The role of the mentor is to accompany in the identification of development challenges, to anchor them in projects and to follow-up on them in a disciplined manner.
   If you can count on the assistance of a mentor, whether it is your boss or someone external to the organisation, his or her role is to accompany you for a reasonable period of time in order to help you to identify your development challenges, to select the competencies (sets of habitual behaviour,

observable and measurable) with which to achieve them, to anchor those competencies in specific projects and to implement them with discipline. Hierarchy alone, however, is not a sufficient qualification for being a mentor. In order to perform the role legitimately, years of disciplined work are necessary, in which head, heart and hands have been applied to the mentor's own development.

3. The three responsibilities of a leader are strategy, people development and day to day operations.
   The difference between mere managers and leaders is that the former focuses all their energy on day to day operations, whereas the latter includes in their agenda the other two responsibilities: strategy and people development. And this difference gives rise to a surprising disparity between being under the control of a manager who fosters your development for purely technical and transactional motives—such as carrying out operational tasks or occupying a position in an organisation structure—or progressing in self-development accompanied by a leader with mentoring skills and a genuine interest in your personal and professional growth.

4. There are two unmistakable indicators of the presence of a leader: They mentor and they give feedback.
   A good indicator of leadership is the capacity to implement an ethos of mentoring and self-development within the leader's own team. And another is the quantity and quality of the feedback given to the boss, to peers, to the immediate team and to anyone else in the organisation, independently of hierarchy, but outside and beyond the organised process of performance evaluation, which is devised mainly to justify the bonus distributed at the end of the year. When you observe in a person that both indicators (mentoring and feedback) are low, the likelihood is that he or she is a

131

manager, with a technical formation and orientated towards getting things done, rather than developing people.

5. Personal transformation is a process of developing habits and character building.

   A personal transformation is not achieved by attending courses, doing programmes or obtaining certificates, like getting stamps in a passport. That, alone, is academic tourism. Nor is it achieved by listening to motivational talks. Rather, people are transformed through learning by doing, from the daily exercise of the will, by developing good habits and building the character that is required for assuming the responsibilities of leadership—irrespectively of whether it is in an organisation of a hundred thousand people or something much more important, in your own family.

6. The quality of the intellectual diet determines the level of leadership.

   The leaders of any organisation, regardless of the sector, do not spend their time manufacturing things. Their performance does not depend on the strength of their arms or their capacity to carry a heavy load on their back. Rather, they spend their time «mindfacturing». So the level of their leadership depends directly on the vitality of their intellect; on their conceptual affluence; on their capacity to process and to synthesise complex information; on their capacity to think critically and not be drawn by superficial, populist slogans; on their competencies in communicating both verbally and in writing; on their skill in swiftly «reading» the talent and personality of people; in other words, on their capacity to navigate through the National Geographic of the human spirit. From this point of view, the habit of reading and studying (books and articles, but also videos, podcasts, documentaries, etcetera) are fabulous tools of personal growth. Today, however, we run the risk of reducing our intellectual diet to serials offered by platforms such as Netflix, a potentially addictive, fast-food self-service outlet.

7. Self-development demands a simple methodology.
Experience obstinately shows that, without a method, the rhythm of learning is too slow and intermittent. But the methodology must be simple, which is an unusual characteristic in large organisations, which tend to fall into over-engineering. And this systemic tendency towards complexity, together with the genuine concern of human resources departments about the lack of implication of many senior managers with regard to people development, ends up producing models for managing talent that are extraordinarily complex and extraordinarily expensive because, without addressing the underlying cause, they try to assume a responsibility that those senior managers have outsourced improperly.

8. Self-development accelerates when it adopts a collaborative approach.
In the last few decades, the constant technological advances have opened up unsuspected possibilities for communication and collaboration between different people. However, due to a surprising inertia, the mainstream mentality in respect of human development in organisations continues to be enclosed within individual formats: at best, you only talk about your personal development with your boss or perhaps with someone from human resources. The idea of pursuing a collaborative culture of self-development, such as we propose in our Self-development Programme, is usually met with initial reticence, based on the axiom that people are not comfortable talking about their development challenges in front of their colleagues. But experience demonstrates time and time again that initial scepticism is followed by positive astonishment at the value of collective conversation for

sharing development challenges and experiences and also learning resources, both through workshops and digital platforms.

9. When evaluating development programmes, it is more important to measure the impact on participants than their satisfaction with the facilitator.
Both in the case of leadership programmes run by human resources departments and those offered by business schools, the current disproportionate emphasis on measuring the participants' satisfaction through evaluation questionnaires runs the risk of becoming a perverse incentive for facilitators and professors to articulate their teaching dynamics so as to entertain their audiences rather than to contribute to the transformation of each person. It is much more important, however, to evaluate the performance of each participant from the perspective of the facilitator or the professor, and also from the perspective of their own colleagues.

10. Transformation hurts.
In the same way as keeping a strict diet or going through a tough physical training programme, transformation hurts. For this reason, the role of the mentor is not to win a popularity contest or to ensure that those who are mentored feel comfortable. Just the opposite. It consists of challenging them—in the most inspiring way possible—and creating a blend of discomfort and of confidence that will inspire them to develop with discipline their own talent.

The Mentoring Process

The experience of having implemented our Self-development Programme in companies from different sectors and from different cultures and continents has allowed us to identify a series of critical moments in the *mentoring* process. We summarise below some of the things we have learned through the implementation of the Self-development Programme we run at **emergap**, which lasts for nine months:

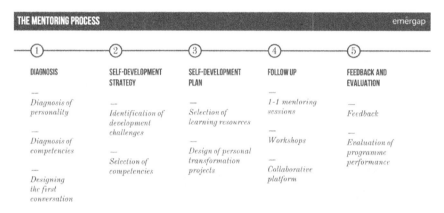

THE MENTORING PROCESS				emergap
①	②	③	④	⑤
DIAGNOSIS	SELF-DEVELOPMENT STRATEGY	SELF-DEVELOPMENT PLAN	FOLLOW UP	FEEDBACK AND EVALUATION
Diagnosis of personality	—	—	*1-1 mentoring sessions*	—
	Identification of development challenges	*Selection of learning resources*		*Feedback*
Diagnosis of competencies	—	—	*Workshops*	*Evaluation of programme performance*
	Selection of competencies	*Design of personal transformation projects*	—	
Designing the first conversation			*Collaborative platform*	

1) DIAGNOSIS

- Diagnosis of personality

  In order to accompany a person through a process of mentoring, it is essential to get to know that person with a certain degree of depth. There are simple tools and models, such as the DISC or the MTBI, which facilitate the identification of traits that are typically found in different personalities.

  These are not mathematical models and should be used prudently, for two reasons. Firstly, when using self-

135

diagnosing personality tests, lack of self-knowledge can on occasions lead to unrealistic answers to questions and, consequently, to results that falsify the conclusions with regard to different types of personality. Secondly, a human being is far more precious and complex than any of these models. Even so, they can be of great help to get to know each person better, to understand their behaviour and to orientate their mentoring process, particularly after using them hundreds of times and having experimented how easy it is to jump to premature conclusions about personality and to label people somewhat frivolously, like using a #hasthtag.

- Diagnosis of competencies
At emergap we have identified twelve "Transformation Competencies" which in our experience are decisive in order to drive change with speed and in depth. Why?

In any organisation there are three dynamics that articulate practically all its activity: personal conversations, collective conversations (or meetings) and communication through digital tools. These twelve competencies, in different degrees, impact the quality in these three environments, which become particularly critical in transformation processes.

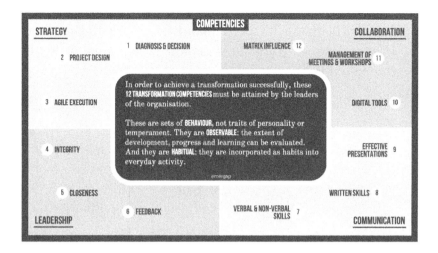

Over the years, we have seen how this model, far from "competing" with those of the organisations we serve, works as an effective complement and offers leaders a framework from which to develop their capacity to transform.

The possession of a model of competencies is a key step in orientating the task of self-development. But unless people experience a certain degree of discomfort and perceive an occasion to make significant improvement, it is unlikely that they will throw themselves into the task of acquiring a competency with method and discipline. To achieve it, a well-sharpened instrument of diagnosis should be used, which describes specific sets of behaviour which defy the person and leave little room for self-complacency, that state of mediocrity which is less painless to accommodate to when you perceive that others are worse off than you. This is the logic of the evaluation instrument[1] that we use at emergap. And a good sign of how well it «cuts» are the remarks

1 https://emergap.com/en/diagnosis/

frequently made by participants in the Self-Development Programme; «I thought I handled meetings well until I completed the competency assessment».

One of the factors that helps to create discomfort in self-diagnosis is the use of a scale with four points (4 Excellent – 3 Good – 2 Average – 1 Bad). On a scale with five points, for example, it is easy to fall into the temptation of giving yourself a mark of 3, the halfway figure, which is not sufficiently uncomfortable and can cloak mediocrity.

- Designing the first conversation
  A mentoring programme is a process that has a greater impact if it begins and ends on a specific date. For this reason, the first conversation is critical in establishing the mechanics, clarifying expectations and setting commitments. If the mentor and the mentee do not know each other, the first conversation is also an opportunity for the mentor to launch a battery of questions that help to "read" the personality and the talent of the mentee and to understand his or her professional and personal context.

  If, on the other hand, they already know each other, but there is a traditional relationship of hierarchy between a manager and a member of his or her team, it is crucial that the first conversation reframes that relationship by focusing exclusively on development and avoiding any mention of day to day work.

2) SELF-DEVELOPMENT STRATEGY

- **Identification of development challenges**
  The first phase of the interaction between mentor and mentee should serve to help to identify development challenges or, to say it in another way, the strategic

priorities for unfurling and deploying talent. And in the same manner as the strategic priorities of a company work when they are few and clearly stated, development challenges should be brief, sharp and easy to remember. In order to identify them correctly, the personality and the professional and personal context of the mentee should be taken into account.

- **Selection of competencies**
  After the development challenges, it is appropriate to select three or four competencies which should be significantly improved during the programme. And it is almost always more practical to begin to work only on one for a period of sixty or ninety days. In any case, competencies are like cherries: you pick one and three or four more come with it. So, while working on one, certain aspects of others can be improved.

3) SELF-DEVELOPMENT PLAN

- **Selection of learning resources**
  This phase is decisive for widening the vision of the mentee and to readjust his or her own perceived level of excellence when working on acquiring a competency. The mentor's own criterion can help to identify an initial selection of books, articles, videos, podcasts, etcetera, depending on the learning style and the gaps in the intellectual diet. Following this initial phase of study, responsibility should be passed on to the mentee to explore further learning resources in accordance with his or her interests and needs.

- **Design of personal transformation projects**
  Until a personal transformation project in respect of a specific competency has been designed, development moves between the head (reflections) and the heart (wishes) of the

mentee. Surprisingly, people with considerable professional experience are frequently found who have difficulty in being specific with these projects, «taking them to the hands», precisely because of their poor development of the competency Project Design. In general, the first version is usually «stratospheric» and requires an early review in order to bring it down to earth.

At **emergap** we have designed a "Personal Transformation Project" template, which fits on a single page to make it simple and easy to remember. In the course of the book, several projects have appeared. Let's take the following one as an example.

These are our recommendations for completing the template:

- Make a very incisive diagnosis of the **Problem/Opportunity**.
- Define a **General Objective** that pursues the strategy of the competency, trying to respond to the development challenges the person faces.
- Define **Specific Objectives** that are sufficiently specific to be able to evaluate their progress from week to week.
- Establish a **Time Frame** for the project of sixty or ninety days. If it is necessary to extend it, successive periods of thirty days may be added.
- Specify several daily and weekly mechanisms of **Implementation**, linked to your personal and professional daily activity.
- And, as part of the implementation, work out an ambitious and demanding study plan. Your **Learning Resources** can include books, articles, podcasts, videos, etc.

4) **FOLLOW-UP**

- **1-1 mentoring sessions**
  Mentoring sessions with the participants in the Self-development Programme have proved to be a particularly effective tool for accelerating and giving more depth to development, both professional and personal. A monthly session of 45 minutes (either face to face or by videoconference) allows for a review of development commitments established in the previous session and to establish new commitments until the next session.

  A healthy combination of discipline to review progress and flexibility to let the conversation flow opens the possibility of establishing both a respectful and a close connection between the mentor and the mentee, such that gives rise to astonishment at the capacity of transformation of the human person.

- **Workshops**
  A bimonthly workshop for the collective follow-up of the transformation projects of each participant in the Self-development Programme is a fascinating experience of collaborative learning. Some people find it hard to believe that others are willing to show their weak points in front of professional colleagues by talking about their development experiences, and even find inconceivable that they should do so in front of their team or their bosses. But the fact is that time and time again traditional talent management paradigms fall apart. Of course, such "magic" does not happen by simply shutting people in a room and obliging them to open up their casket of intimacy. The proper climate has to be created, which requires having developed competencies to facilitate this kind of workshop and to gain the trust and respect of the participants, as a result of

experience and of a genuine aspiration to serve them.

- **Collaborative platform**

  Another surprising tool that accelerates people's development is opening a private channel on a digital platform (Workplace, Yammer, Teams or LinkedIn, for example) so that learning resources and experiences may be shared permanently between the participants of the Self-development Programme. To start this up, an initial commitment must be made to publish at least once a week a self-development learning experience which may enrich the other participants in the programme.

  Experience shows that the impact of this tool is directly proportional to the importance attached to it by members of the management team who participate in the Self-development Programme, and who thus lead by example. If they are the first to publish their progress and contribute learning resources, they send an unambiguous message that self-development is a strategic priority for the company. And when this example is sustained over time, a new capacity becomes installed in the company, self-development, which is particularly critical in times of transformation.

5) FEEDBACK AND EVALUATION

- **Feedback**

  In addition to moments of personal feedback provided by the Self-development Programme (1-1 mentoring sessions) and group sessions (follow-up workshops), the mere fact of working with method and with discipline on the development of their own competencies leads to the effort of participants inevitably manifesting itself in the context of their daily work and also in their private lives. These environments provide opportunities to ask for feedback on progress in development from colleagues at work or from the family. By taking advantage of this feedback they become opportunities to enrich perspectives and to find motivation to continue.

- **Evaluation of performance on the programme**
  An easy way to evaluate the performance of the participants in the Self-development Programme is to ask them, at the end of the programme, to evaluate themselves and each other (using the scale: 4 Excellent - 3 Good – 2 Average – 1 Bad) in two variables: first, the degree of development of competencies during the programme and, second, the degree of discipline observed in their self-development. In addition, these two evaluations (How do I see myself? And how do my colleagues see me?) are appraised by our evaluation as mentors.

The cross-assessment of these three perspectives provides quite a sharp diagnosis of the people with greatest growth potential, both in the organisation and in their own lives. Below, we give an example of the performance evaluation of a group of high potentials who went through the programme.

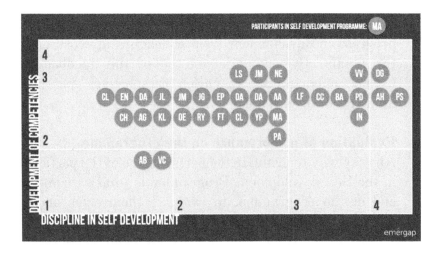

The following table shows how the different activities of the Self-Development Programme are integrated into an annual calendar.

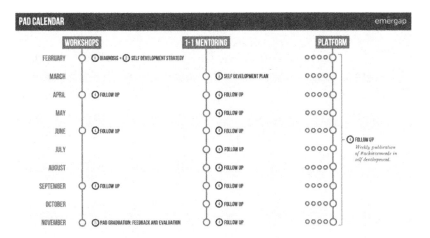

Learning Resources

This chapter brings together the learning resources that have been mentioned in the course of the book, during the interaction between Oliver and Sarah. It is by no means an exhaustive list, but a short range of resources we suggest during the Programme.

Books

Crime and Punishment. Fyodor Dostoyevsky
Delegating Work. HBR Press
Empathy. HBR Press
Focus. Cal Newport
Getting Work Done. HBR Press
Leading Virtual Teams. HBR Press
Man's Search for Meaning. Viktor E. Frankl
Managing Time. HBR Press
Mindsight. Daniel J Siegel
Nicomachean Ethics. Aristotle
Open. Andre Agassi
Seven Habits. Stephen R. Covey
The Digital Transformation Playbook. David L. Rogers
The Power of Habit. Charles Duhigg
The Speed of Trust. Stephen R. Covey
Thinking, Fast and Slow. Daniel Kahneman
Ultralearning. Scott H. Young
Unbeatable Mind. Mark Divine
Unbroken. Laura Hillenbrand
Virtual Collaboration. HBR Press
Wild at Heart. John Eldredge
Wounds in the Heart. Javier Schlatter

Articles
Are You Ready to Decide? McKinsey Quarterly
How Social Tools Can Reshape the Organization. Digital McKinsey
How to Make your Company Smarter: Decision Making. MITSloan Management Review

Videos
TED | *5 Ways to Listen Better.*
TED | *El poder de la conversación.*
YouTube | *How to Really Listen to People.*
YouTube | *Optimal Work.*
Netflix | *Tidying up with Marie Kondo!*

Apps
Audible
Habitify
Grammarly
Workplace

Links
Center for Creative Leadership | Feedback technique SCI | *bit.ly/ccym-sci*
Diagnosis of Transformation Competencies | *emergap.com/diagnosis*
Test de personality DISC | *mydiscprofile.com/es-es/*
The Definitive 100 Most Useful Productivity Hacks | *bit.ly/ccym-100ph*

The Challenge of the #BridgeGeneration

If you have this book in your hands, you are probably a member of the *#BridgeGeneration*, who crossed the bridge from an analogical to a digital world. Perhaps you crossed in short trousers, playing distractedly, or perhaps you crossed with the weight and giddiness of responsibility on your shoulders. Now that we are on this side—sometimes fascinated by the transformations that technology brings when it combines with creativity, and sometimes overwhelmed by the anxiety that hyper connectivity arouses in us—let's stop and think for a moment.

We have lived through a fascinating period of the history of mankind. Never before has any generation had to learn so many things in so little time. But although many companies and educational institutions have created training and educational programmes aimed at acquiring knowledge and developing skills, there is no challenge comparable to the building of your character, to acquiring that «inner weight» and depth of character that allows you to face your family, your friends and your colleagues, and constantly enjoin them to make extraordinary efforts to give their full potential; not from a life without blemish, cold and aloof, but from the inspiring example of a life of struggle that is conscious of its own fragility.

It is possible that, for years, in spite of the multitude that besieges you in your work and from digital platforms, you have travelled the journey of your development alone. If this is the case, I would like to make you a suggestion: look for mentors to accompany you on each stage of your journey, and who inspire you to keep growing day by day. With time, perhaps when your body has lost the vigour of youth, you will discover a tremendous strength inside that will attract others to invite you into their lives, into their journey of transformation.

Acknowledgements

First and foremost, my thanks to Alejandro Mesa, who lent me his country house in Llanogrande to get this book started. And, above all, for allowing me to get to know his family and for granting me the gift of his friends. They are now also mine.

And thank you to all those who with their feedback have helped me to polish the book:

Andrea Escobar, Andrés Acosta, Andrés Arango, Borja de León, Carlos Eduardo Mesa, Carolina Acosta, Carolina García, César Suárez, Claire French, Claus Flensborg, David Gallagher, Diego Fontán, Elena Mesonero, Emilio Iturmendi, Ernesto Barrera, Esteban Betancur, Francisco Fernández, Gonzalo Valseca, Guillermo Arroyo, Íñigo Pírfano, Joaquín Trigueros, John Almandoz, José María Díez, Juan Beltrán, Juan José Valle, Juan Carlos Valverde, Juan Pablo Murra, Kleverson Batistela, Linc Holt Wilgaard, Lisa Le Vere, Luis Casas, Luis Ignacio Franco, Maca Lalinde, Margara Ferber, Mike Roche, Nathan Davis, Paloma Martínez, Rafael García, Rolando Roncancio, Sergio Pardo, Valeria Fratocchi and Xavier Bosch.

Comments on the Book

Alejandro Mesa | Chairman of Premex
"A masterful invitation to become the protagonists accountable for our own self-development, through a familiar story, deep and inspiring, with a methodology that is simple, well-proven and transforming."

Carlos Zenteno | Chairman of Claro (Colombia)
"An exceptional book. Through a story that could well be that of many professional people who have not discovered the path that leads to their full development, Alvaro leads us by the hand through a process of practical, simple and structured learning, imbued with humanism, which will undoubtedly leave its mark on a large number of people."

David Garza | President of TEC of Monterrey
"In this different, agreeable and revealing text, Alvaro takes us into deep reflections, at the same time as practical considerations, of what is required to be a transformational leader. The model for transformation competencies, the methodology for self-development, the necessary emphasis on discipline and, particularly, the humanist focus, make it different from other books on leadership. Understanding it, loving it and doing it, will remain with the reader all his life."

Santiago Zapata | General Manager, HiCue Speakers

"The perfect book for anyone who wants to initiate a process of true personal transformation, following a methodology that is clear, simple and easily implemented. By means of a deep but enjoyable conversation, that feels that it might be taking place in your own home, Alvaro leads us by the hand on a fascinating journey of transformation, helping us to develop new competencies."

Carlos Rodríguez de Robles | Deputy CEO at CACEIS
"With a humanist approach, based on the integrality of the human person, Alvaro provides us in this book with a story of a personal transformation by means of a methodology that is simple but also demanding, and which undoubtedly contributes to our personal growth and to being able to contribute to the growth of the people around us."

Ignacio Calle | Chairman of SURA Asset Management
"In this book, Alvaro provides us with a valuable work log. With the use of a practical methodology, it gives rise to a personal transformation in leaders and people with high potential. It is a creatively written and allows us to encroach on the privacy of the characters from the perspective of both the mentor and the person he accompanies in her transformation."

Juan David Correa | CEO of Protección
"The process of personal and professional development of human beings is a commitment and a conviction that lasts for the rest of life. This book is a guide that provokes reflection and, as a consequence of experience and of tools that are simple to use, it leads to putting into practice those actions that bring about a true transformation."

Pablo Sprenger | CEO SURA Investment Management
"It doesn't matter whether you are a senior executive or are starting your professional career, this book is required reading

to equip yourself with better tools to face the challenging and competitive world we live in. Through the use of a fascinating story, Alvaro admirably manages to inspire the reader to commit head, heart and hands to his own self-development, which is undoubtedly the new competitive difference of the leaders of the future."

Carlos Raúl Yepes | Ex Chairman of Bancolombia
"Just reading the title reveals what Alvaro intends to transmit to us with this book: a message for our personal and professional life which passes unfailingly through our head, our heart and our hands. The head that thinks, the heart that feels and the hands that all in unity build a better human being at the service of organisations and of society. This book puts forward a new and attractive outlook which very significantly makes us think and provides us with valuable tools for action."

Montserrat Garrido | Sales Manager Transaction Banking Latin America at Citi
"Technology is changing organisations at an exponential rate. However, only if leaders learn how to contribute to transforming people, they will be able to inspire others and to attract the best. With an engaging and warm-hearted style and a practical methodology, this book invites us to begin at home, with ourselves, so that a transformation can have a real impact on our organisations and on our environment."

Carolina Acosta | Country Representative of the University of Navarre in Colombia
"The book has made me laugh, has made me cry and has made me confront myself."

Claus Flensborg | Director of Global Learning and Development at Arla Foods

"Read it—just read it! The personal transformation story is fascinating, and the methodology is simple and powerful".

Claire French | Director of Bonida Consulting
"Transformation is key to our lives and this book provides a simple and effective methodology woven into a wonderful story. The gift of this book is that Álvaro has illustrated how realistic and practical the methodology is to use through the dialogue between Sarah and Oliver. A must read for every leader!".

James Pampillón | Manager, Sales Development EMEA Growth Markets at Salesforce
"I read this book in two sittings. I completely identify with the main character and her way of dealing with issues in her professional and personal life. This book has taught me the importance of having someone who can challenge you and provide perspective, knowing that it is ultimately up to you personally to want to change. But for this you need a proper methodology, time for reflection and discipline."

Monsterrat Ezquerra | Global Human Resources Manager at Santander Bank

Made in United States
Orlando, FL
17 August 2022

21094071R00096